A SENSE OF VALUES

A Sense of Values
American Warriors in an Uncertain World

David Bowne Wood

Photographs by Bob Mahoney

Andrews and McMeel
A Universal Press Syndicate Company
Kansas City

Design by Ed King with page layout by Charles W. King

Library of Congress Cataloging-in-Publication Data

Wood, David Bowne.
        A sense of values : American Marines in an
uncertain world /
 David Bowne Wood : photographs by Bob Mahoney.
                p.   cm.
        ISBN 0-8362-8073-3 : $24.95
        1. United States. Marine Corps. Marine Expedi-
tionary Unit, Special Operations Capable, 24th.
2. Operation Restore Hope, 1992–1993.   I. Mahoney,
Bob. II. Title.
VE23.W66   1994
359.9'63'0973—dc20   94-27260
                                        CIP

For our families and colleagues.

They encouraged us to go

and sustained us while we were away,

and graciously welcomed us back.

Contents

A SENSE OF VALUES

Hovercraft comes ashore from USS *Wasp*, background.

Prologue

Marines are a familiar part of America.

They are cultural icons, like cops or pro football players. Marines occasionally appear on TV news. You see them lining up on a runway, getting ready to board a plane to some godforsaken place. You see a smartly uniformed Marine assisting the president down from his helicopter on the White House lawn. Marine bands and precision drill teams thrill crowds along parade routes.

Marines are warriors, a profession Americans have always looked upon with awe and distrust.

In the caricature favored by cartoonists and Hollywood screenwriters, Marines are big and brawny and brave. Maybe not so smart. They chew cigars and knock heads. The few, the proud.

Tough guys.

Few outsiders see beyond this fiction.

The Marine Corps is a brotherhood (only one of twenty Marines is a woman; none of them currently serve in combat positions). Marines divide the world into two classes: Marines, and those who aren't good enough to be Marines. They live isolated lives, cloistered in timeless rituals and bent to service like monks of an austere sect.

And when the nation needs them, they go. Today's fashionable notions of peacekeeping and crisis-intervention are old stories to Marines. So are big, bloody wars—the popular ones and the unpopular ones. Since 1945, Marines have been sent about twice a year to resolve some distant U.S. foreign-policy problem.

They go, and most come back, and only rarely does the nation notice. Even less does the nation participate. In 1993, fewer than eight in a thousand eighteen-to-twenty-four-year-old Americans volunteered for military service. Only about one in a thousand made it into the Marines.

These numbers are troubling. They mark the growing distance between America and its military—a gap of unshared experience and, perhaps, unshared values.

No one suggests that the nation needs more Marines, or that military service should be required of all young Americans. And yet, a crucial principle lies at the heart of America's 218-year-old experiment in participatory democracy: the connection between citizenship and service and nation. In this last decade of the twentieth century, that connection seems to be dissolving.

It was an attempt to explore these questions that put me on a Somali beach amid the bedlam of a Marine amphibious landing. Who are these guys? Where do they come from, and why? And what's it like with them
out there?

Colonel Matthew Broderick looked surprised and pleased to see me there.

Broderick had come with his force of 2,100 Marines, sailing from Camp Lejeune, North Carolina, in four warships now anchored off the Somali coast. I had flown from Washington, D.C., to Nairobi, catching a

Colonel Matthew Broderick, center.

Marines of the 24th MEU come ashore, Mogadishu.

ride into Somalia on a single-engine plane chartered by a relief agency. We hadn't seen each other for a month, and he wasn't sure I would actually show up.

We stood for a few moments savoring the crashing din around us. Despite the sultry heat, Broderick wore full-length, mottled brown and tan desert camouflage utilities, helmet, and a 9-mm pistol strapped across his chest. (Army troops and Marines wear identical combat uniforms. The Army calls them "fatigues"; Marines call them "utilities.")

A few yards away, heavy trucks and massive armored vehicles were grinding down the ramp of a huge Hovercraft that had just slewed up on the rocky beach. Offshore, beyond a line of breaking surf, another Hovercraft was headed in from the amphibious assault carrier USS *Wasp* lying on the horizon. Laden with sixty tons of cargo, the Hovercraft came bouncing toward us over the aqua sea, its turbine engines shrieking at seventy-five thousand horsepower and whipping up a typhoon of spray and exhaust. Combat-laden Marines trudged across the damp sand, lugging machine guns and stretchers and radios and jerry cans of fuel and water, straining and blinking away the sweat trickling down from under their helmets. Armored vehicles lurched and churned across the dunes. Platoon sergeants bellowed. The sun burned down from a clear sky. Flags snapped in the breeze.

It was a fine day, the twenty-fourth of March, 1993.

For someone who grew up poor in the town of Westborough, Mass., Matthew Broderick had come a long way. As a kid, he picked up bundled newspapers at the train station well after midnight, fighting off the drunks who stumbled out of the local bars to get the early racing results. He worked full time while going to college. In 1967, Broderick left his job practice-teaching junior high school history and geography, shucked his draft deferment, and joined the Marines. In Vietnam he was decorated for heroism under fire. At the war's end, he told himself he'd go back to teaching when he stopped having fun.

Two decades later, Broderick is a colonel, United States Marine Corps. He is the commanding officer of the 24th Marine Expeditionary Unit, a self-contained force of twenty-one hundred men with enough firepower (attack jets, helicopter gunships, artillery, infantry) to make a tin-pot dictator blink with tears of envy.

The Marine Corps is not in the practice of casually handing over responsibility for such a force to just anyone who comes up through the ranks. Unlike Army or Air Force fighting units of similar size, Marine expeditionary units do not ordinarily operate alongside a larger force. Often, they operate independently and alone in the world's bad neighborhoods, far out on the periphery of American power. All of the men, and especially their commander, must be tough, smart, and professional.

There are 642 colonels in the Marine Corps. Six are selected to command Marine expeditionary units. They are exceptional men.

In the little more than six months that Broderick has held command, he has put his personal stamp on this force. Back home at Camp Lejeune, he has rammed his men through months of exhausting training. His officers and senior enlisted men have had to earn his trust. They do things Broderick's way, and they do them perfectly. Down to the level of the lowliest private, Broderick's Marines struggle and curse and vow to quit when this is all over, but they perform, and in the end they love him for it, and they are proud to be Marines.

The Marine Corps and I had struck an unusual deal. They would take me in, but not for the one- or two-day snapshot usually allowed a visiting reporter. This would take much of a year. In return, photographer Bob Mahoney and I, as part of my regular reporting as the national security correspondent for Newhouse News Service, would have total access to the 24th Marine Expeditionary Unit for an unvarnished, "warts-and-all" portrait of Broderick, his men, and their mission.

We came together from wildly divergent backgrounds. Over half of Broderick's men came from families in which at least one parent had done military service. All the men had survived the brutality of enlisted boot camp (or the equally rigorous officers' version of boot camp), and had been polished over years of additional schooling and training.

I grew up in a pacifist family. As a conscientious objector during the Vietnam War, I did two years of national service in place of military duty. I earned a degree in journalism and African history, and wandered the globe for twenty years as a newsmagazine and newspaper correspondent. I covered enough wars for a lifetime, but always as an outsider.

By the time we got to Somalia, I had been through weeks of Broderick's training.

I had watched Mark Toal, one of Broderick's young captains, struggle to meet the colonel's demanding expectations.

I had stood guard duty with the born-again Eddie Adams, a tall Alabaman with high hopes and deep fears about the mission to Somalia.

I'd suffered with Jose Rocha, a chunky kid from Miami, as our helicopter lurched and bucked through a windy sky, and I'd sat with "Mad Dog" Moore as he deftly guided his helo down into a tiny landing zone.

I'd gone down an icy river in a small rubber boat at midnight on an exercise raid with Norman North, and we'd been teargassed together in a mock ambush.

And I had talked over the joys and hassles of bringing up a family with George Fenton, Broderick's operations officer, and with Steve McGowin, an intelligence analyst.

I turned forty-eight years old with the Marines in Somalia, and I had to work at keeping up with physical fitness fanatics half my age. Broderick and Fenton and Rocha and Adams and Toal cut me no slack: I could go with them, or not. I could watch comfortably and safely from the sidelines, or I could go with them and share the risk, the discomfort, and the rewards.

I went.

They made room for me. They shared their chow, their precious bunk space, and their combat gear with me. They took me along on their physical training runs, and included me in their practical jokes. They patiently fielded my questions, shared their deepest confidences, and opened their families to me as well. They took the time to fill out the detailed, anonymous questionnaires that I gave each one (the data is incorporated in the book, and the lengthy comments that many Marines added are scattered throughout).

We shared long days of grueling physical exertion, long days of grinding boredom, and a few moments of fear. While I was busy taking notes, they covered my back.

Philosophically, we came to the business of war from radically different angles. But here, too, we found comfortable common ground, for there are no advocates of peace more sincere than those sworn to offer their lives in war.

After many months with the Marines, I thought I had successfully crossed that wide divide between my civilian world and their military one. Until one night on board the Marines' flagship, the USS *Wasp*, off the coast of Somalia. The following morning the Marines would steam away to the Persian Gulf, and I was trying to figure out how to get back to Washington. I sought the help of Gunnery Sergeant Willie Porter, the Marines' highly capable paperwork czar.

Me: "Hey Gunny, there's a C-141 [U.S. military transport plane] leaving Mogadishu tomorrow. Can you get me on it?"

Gunny: "Sure, no sweat. I'll just stamp your orders."

Me: "Orders? I don't have any orders. I'm not a Marine, remember?"

Gunny: "No . . . orders? [Smiles in disbelief, as if I had said I have no bellybutton.] No orders? Then how'd you get here?"

Me: "747 and a Cessna."

Gunny: "No, I mean who gave you permission?"

Me: "Well, I guess the headquarters of the Marine Corps . . . the commandant of the Marine Corps."

Gunny (Triumphantly): "Well, okay! Lemme see the orders."

Me: "Gunny, there aren't any orders. I just came."

Gunny: "Well, I don't know how you got out here with no orders. But you're sure as hell not going out of here with no orders."

The next morning, I hitched a ride out of Mogadishu on a United Nations plane.

Civilians cannot and will not understand us because they are not one of us. The Corps—we love it, live it, and shall die for it. If you have never been in it you shall never understand it. Semper Fidelis!
—Lance Corporal, Mortars

I swore to defend my nation against all enemies foreign and domestic. It doesn't get any simpler. Stop trying to understand us. We are all multifaceted people, not military clones.
—Corporal, Logistics

You've been with us the whole float and you've seen the bullshit we go through. So don't be like all the other authors who write about the military and lie their ass off. . . . Thanks for being there, it takes a lot of balls to go into a place like Somalia without a weapon. But just remember we always had your back covered.
—Corporal, Amphibious Assault Vehicles

1

PURPLE BEACH
SOUTHERN SOMALIA
March 1993

On a dark, windswept shore thousands of miles from home, a few dozen young Americans gather for an impromptu prayer meeting. They draw close, resting their rifle butts in the damp sand and cradling their helmets in their arms. The immense, starry stillness of the sultry African night seems to press down on their bare heads. From out of the darkness comes the distant clang of a wrench on metal, a muffled curse, the squeak of a wooden ammunition crate being pried open—counterpoints to the steady sigh of the wind and the indistinct rumble of heavy armored vehicles waiting at idle.

Further out there in the darkness, beyond these comfortably familiar sounds, awaits an alien landscape of destruction and death.

The soft wind carries the scent of Somalia's wretched, centuries-old poverty and dust and hopelessness. The wind carries a newer scent, too, of man's own capacity for brutality. This scent hints of ashes, blasted rubble, rotting corpses. It flows from distant, deserted streets and from buildings that human beings have bombed and rocketed and machine-gunned and bombed again, and then looted and burned, and machine-gunned again for good measure.

Generations of Somalis molder in mass graves; some lie unburied and unrecognizable in forgotten alleyways. The dazed, walking wounded who survive haunt the shadows of the land, carrying weapons and an inexplicable, burning resentment. They have vowed to kill outsiders who stand in their way, and they have made good on the threat.

The young Americans on the beach are United States Marines. They have been dispatched here by politicians, egged on by foreign-policy experts and

Somali kids, Purple Beach.

editorial writers, on a convulsive wave of goodwill and idealism: Somalis are starving. We're Americans. We can fix it.

On a brutally hot day, the Marines have stormed ashore in a ferocious thunder of helicopters and air-cushion landing craft, wrestling armored vehicles and ammunition and fuel across the sand to form up a combat convoy. Now, hours after dark has fallen, the Marines are sun-dazed and exhausted, snatching a few hours of quiet before they begin the assault into Somalia.

Norman North, a tall, lean man with a dashing Errol Flynn mustache, squats on the sand in the pitch black. He is a staff sergeant, and he is using his dozen years of Marine Corps experience to make field coffee. He has carefully collected a few sticks and lovingly erected them over a lit piece of paper torn from his notebook. He slides his canteen off his web gear, extracts the aluminum cup, and starts dumping in ingredients scrounged from several bulky brown plastic field-rations packages— Meals, Ready to Eat, or MREs.

Four packets of Taster's Choice instant coffee. One packet of instant creamer. Five packets of sugar. He tops it up with water, stirs it dubiously with his knife, and sets it on the blaze. Soon, acrid fumes begin to rise from the cup. "Gah-*damn!*" he says feelingly. He lights up a Kool with a snap of his Zippo lighter, rocks back on his heels, and sighs contentedly.

From out of the darkness comes an incongruous and eerie sound. Muffled by the gusting wind, the male voices are lifted in the haunting strains of "Amazing Grace." As the faint voices rise and fall, Staff Sergeant North lifts his coffee from the fire. "Enjoy it while you can," he says to a companion. "Ain't gonna be much time for this later on."

North leans back on the damp sand. His mind is wandering back a

Purple Beach.

decade when this same unit of Marines—the 24th Marine Expeditionary Unit—was grabbing a few hours rest in a temporary bivouac, a four-story concrete building at the edge of the international airport in Beirut, Lebanon. The Marines had been sent there, on a wave of goodwill and idealism, to bring peace to an unpeaceful place. Some people resented them being there. At 6:22 in the morning of October 23, 1983, a terrorist bomb exploded, blasting American idealism into shreds.

Two hundred and twenty young Marines and sailors were killed. One hundred wounded were dug out of the rubble. Some of the survivors came home with deep psychological scars of horror. And with an abiding disgust for the politicians who had sent them on an ill-defined peacekeeping mission and tied their hands with political restrictions that got them bogged down in a nasty war with no way to defend themselves.

Tonight on this windswept beach in Somalia, some Marines are privately worried that Somalia is going to be Beirut all over again. That once again they've been thoughtlessly thrown at a problem by politicians who understand neither the problem nor the military force they have sent to fix it. Tonight, as on that grim dawn ten years ago, the politicians who issued the Marines their orders are far behind. Now it is up to these young Americans.

For here—by North's guttering fire, and a few hundred yards down the beach where Marines are singing, and up the hill where Donald Mortimer is packing bullets into ammo magazines and Jon Flores and Michael Bowlin are fixing an oil leak on their vehicle—here is the far edge of America's power.

Back in Washington and New York, policy analysts and editorial writers and TV producers and poll-takers and decision-makers have deliberated in the grandeur of marble and mahogany, have made their decisions, and have gone on to preen on television talk shows and at high-toned dinner parties.

Out here is where their good intentions meet reality.

On the shoulders of these Marines rests the fate of American interests and American prestige—American power. They were not participants in the making of U.S. policy in Somalia. They are the implementers. If the policy works, they will win the momentary affection of the public. If it fails, they will pay for it. When these Marines move out into Somalia in a few hours, it will be their reputations, their pride, their idealism—their lives—on the line.

The 24th MEU arriving, Purple Beach.

Most of them are barely out of their teens.

Jose Rocha, playing grab-ass with his buddies from Weapons Company, is an antitank gunner. He's from Miami and he's twenty-four. Steve Neely, a rifleman in Charlie Company, is twenty-three. He grew up in a wealthy neighborhood in Rockville, Md., a suburb of Washington, D.C.

Erik Dacey, twenty-one, is from Flemington, N.J. The only one of his high school class of three hundred who enlisted in the Marines, he will ride into the Somali bush in a few hours inside the sweltering black hull of an Amtrack, a heavily armored troop carrier that rides on treads like a tank.

Dacey, a lance corporal, is holding a flashlight on a map showing the route the Marines will follow. "There are hyenas out there," says his lieutenant. "And yes, they eat people. They've gotten used to feeding off bodies." Dacey chuckles nervously. He is not sure if his lieutenant is kidding or not (he is not).

Donald Mortimer, a staff sergeant, commands a smaller armored troop carrier called a Light Armored Vehicle, or LAV, that rides on oversize tires. His vehicle is called the Hell Bitch. Mortimer, an elder at thirty-six, is from Grass Lake, a small town in upper Michigan. His mechanic, twenty-three-year-old Jon Flores, is from Rockdale, Tex. Michael Bowlin, who drives the Hell Bitch from a cramped cockpit, is twenty-one. He's from Omaha.

Many of them have fled dead-end jobs or stifling families or abortive attempts at college. All of them have fled the commonplace of shopping malls and interstate highways and fast-food drive-ins, seeking instead challenge and excitement, uncommon deeds, valor, glory.

There is something else they seek: the sense of identity, of community, the sense of common principled purpose and the moral certainties that America, they believe, is losing.

In the Marine Corps they find that principle and purpose and community. They are steeped in it from the moment they step off the bus at the Marine Corps recruit depot at Parris Island, South Carolina ("Surrender mind and spirit to harsh instruction and receive a soul," says a sign at Parris Island boot camp). The recruits' reliance on friends and family is ripped away; their passionate visions of glory are honed on the granite-hard virtues of duty, honor, service.

As young Marines, they are burdened with responsibilities far beyond those allowed to their civilian peers. You are responsible for the life of your buddy. No questions, no excuses. On duty and off duty, it is an unforgiving code. It means making sure your buddy masters the three-inch-thick, small-print *Battle Skills Training Handbook*. It means if he gets drunk off-post some night, you get him home. It means if he takes a round in the lung, you can rip a battle dressing out of his first aid kit and save his life because you know how to treat a sucking chest wound.

If you can do all of this and more, you win promotion. Now you are responsible for the four men in your fire team. Those who excel are promoted to heavier responsibilities; those who falter are unceremoniously let go.

Those who are kept are proud, confident, capable, and eager.

Of course, these Marines are armed with more than self-confidence and idealism. There are 2,100 of them here, organized into a floating force the Marines call a Marine expeditionary unit. The United States boasts six such units and deploys them two at a time on rotating six-month "floats."

Each MEU is a microcosm of the combat power of the United States. Each has its own air power, its own artillery, infantry, combat engineers, intelligence units, supply units, medical unit, reconnaissance teams, and even a group of air controllers—a self-contained force packaged for air assaults and amphibious landings.

This one is known as the 24th Marine Expeditionary Unit. Serving in it is such demanding duty that, like the other MEUs, it is disbanded after each float, then reassembled with different parts—a Marine infantry battalion from here, a helicopter squadron from there, an artillery battery from someplace else—and trained for six months before deploying on another float.

In its six months of training, the 24th MEU has rigorously rehearsed difficult and dangerous high-speed operations such as freeing hostages, rescuing airmen downed in hostile territory, and evacuating U.S. civilians from a besieged embassy. At their home base at Camp Lejeune on the North Carolina coast, the Marines have demonstrated these skills to slit-eyed Marine evaluators eager to find a way to fail them. They have passed and won the coveted designation, Special Operations Capable (SOC).

In the peculiar language of the Marines, this outfit is known as "Two Four Mew, Sock."

Twenty-fourth MEU-SOC is organized around a basic infantry battalion containing three companies (Alpha, Bravo, and Charlie). Each is led by a Marine captain, and each company has roughly two hundred Marines.

Since the MEU's infantry battalion will be operating far from reinforcements, it brings its own. It is beefed up with a weapons company armed with antitank weapons, an artillery battery, and an amphibious assault platoon. The MEU also carries its own support group organized into platoons to provide maintenance, communications, engineers (for breaching mine fields or building refugee housing), medical care, truck transportation, and one platoon trained to organize and supervise amphibious beach landings.

Grafted onto this structure is an air squadron of twenty-three transport and attack helicopters, six Harrier fighter-attack aircraft, and the pilots and technicians to keep them all running.

All of these people, their equipment, and vehicles and supplies are loaded onto four ships designed to operate together as a small armada, or what the Navy (which owns and operates the ships) calls an amphibious ready group, or ARG (pronounced "Aaaargggghh"). ARGs can come in all shapes and sizes, depending on the mission. Normally they are composed of amphibious ships, designed to launch small boats and vehicles in shallow water close to shore.

The 24th MEU is loaded onto ARG 2-93 (the military loves acronyms, but they sometimes make sense; ARG 2-93 designates the amphibious ready group that sails in the second month of 1993). The flagship of ARG 2-93 is the USS *Wasp*, an amphibious assault carrier that carries and can launch jet fighter-bombers, helicopters, and air-cushion landing craft.

Commissioned in 1989, *Wasp* is almost brand-new. She is accompanied by the USS *Nashville*, a smaller ship that also launches helicopters and small boats; the USS *Barnstable County*, a flat-bottomed ship designed to drive virtually up on the beach; and the *El Paso*, a cargo ship.

Marines fondly call the *Wasp*, with its Harrier jets, its anti-aircraft missile system and its space-age technology, the "Death Star." The older and smaller *Nashville* is known as the "Nasty." *Barnstable County*, which rolls like a drunken mule even in light seas, is the "Unstable." The *El Paso* is a clunky ship that hauls mostly spare parts. It is so spartan that some of the Marine officers who bunk on the ship have rigged up their office in a large shipping crate lashed down in the hold; they have run in electric lights and air conditioning. The *El Paso* is not graced with a nickname.

Stored in the ships' holds are twenty-two armored vehicles of both the wheeled and tracked types, dump trucks, a bulldozer, fork-lift trucks and Humvees (the modern-day Jeep). These vehicles are crammed in with the Hovercraft, World War II–type landing craft, and a marina's worth of powerful speedboats of various types.

There is enough ammunition for a sixty-day war. For lesser contingencies, the holds are stuffed with lumber and canvas and nails for building emergency shelters, and even baby formula, feminine napkins, and diapers for the families of refugees or evacuees.

Presiding over this vast enterprise is a colonel. More precisely, The Colonel, Matthew E. Broderick.

Broderick is gruff and stocky, a red-haired Irishman. He is the only colonel on board or anywhere in the vicinity. When Broderick's phone rings, he picks it up and barks, "Colonel!" But in the peculiar lexicon of the Navy and Marine Corps, Broderick carries the same official name as his unit. Whenever he comes on board the *Wasp*, the ship's loudspeaker blares: "Arriving! Two Four Mew, Soc!"

Broderick is forty-eight. He has a team of other officers to help run the MEU. A lieutenant colonel (or "light" colonel) commands the battalion. Majors fill jobs as staff department heads (intelligence, operations, logistics). They are identified not by name, but by number. Thus, Major Larry Hamilton, the MEU's prematurely gray-haired intelligence chief, is known as S (for staff) -2. When Broderick barks "S-2!" Larry Hamilton stands up. (Informally, Hamilton is known as "Two." His office is the "two-shop." Even more informally, "intelligence" is known as S-2, as in, "He don't have too much S-2 upstairs, know what I mean?")

Marine captains, in this hierarchy, command Broderick's companies. Captains like Mark Toal, who commands Charlie Company, are usually around thirty years old.

But the vast majority of the men of the 24th MEU are young, twenty-two years or younger. Most of the work and a fair amount of the responsibility falls on them.

In Toal's Charlie Company, for instance, are four platoons (three platoons of riflemen, one weapons platoon with machine guns and mortars). Each platoon has four squads. And each squad has a fire team.

Fire teams, which have three or four men, are the basic units of the Marine Corps. They are led by corporals, who are usually twenty or twenty-one years old and have two or three years of experience. Sometimes, they're led by lance corporals, the next lower rank (one rank above private first class).

Fire teams are intimate and tight. They live in barracks together,

Broderick. Background, Navy Captain Ken Pyle, commodore of the 24th MEU four-warship task force.

they do their morning three-mile run together, and some weekends they drink beer together (and one of them will get them all home safely). In Somalia they will walk night patrols together and will man lonely checkpoints; they will endure taunts and thrown rocks and will protect each other's lives. In Mogadishu, Nicholas Smith will lead his team out of a tight spot and will be decorated. A lance corporal, he is twenty-one.

It is a difficult and exasperating job to assemble all these people and their gear onto the ships and to train them all to work in concert. The reason for doing it is not readily apparent to the Marines who have struggled ashore on Purple Beach today. But it is clear from the vantage point of the Pentagon's command center and the White House's Oval Office.

The United States has other forces—such as the Army's 82nd Airborne Division—that can respond to a crisis in a flash. The 82nd is a fine fighting force, but it doesn't come with its own jet fighters, bulldozers, or much of anything else. Sending the 82nd is a Big Deal that requires hundreds of heavy aircraft flights, a large airport, and time (and permission) to land follow-on forces to support the paratroopers.

In contrast, a couple of MEUs can be positioned around in the world's bad neighborhoods where they float offshore and unseen, ready in case there is trouble. During the long and bloody upheaval in the former Yugoslavia, for instance, a MEU has hung around in the Adriatic Sea in case a downed American pilot or a pinned-down UN peacekeeping patrol has to be rescued.

During the war in Liberia several years ago, a MEU steamed off the West African coast in case it was needed. For ninety long days the Marines, crammed below decks, waited. Then they were needed, quickly. They stormed ashore and airlifted back to their ships several hundred Americans and other diplomats as the capital, Monrovia, was collapsing in bloody chaos.

"Dial 911—we are the world's emergency phone call," grins Michael Rosenberger, a lanky twenty-year-old private first class from Pittsburgh. "Most of the time, though, we sit around," he says ruefully.

While a crisis is building, while diplomats are struggling to avoid having to commit military forces, having a MEU handy is comforting insurance.

"It's hard to lie offshore with a C-141 [transport plane] full of airborne troops," General Colin Powell, former chairman of the Joint Chiefs of Staff, once remarked.

Good as they are, the men of the 24th MEU don't have the firepower of an armored division or the specialized skills of Delta Force, America's premier commando unit. But as Broderick puts it, "You may not have time to call in those national assets. The difference is, we are already here."

Broderick grew up a scrapper in a destitute family. His father was an alcoholic. As a child, Broderick cleaned garbage cans and delivered newspapers to help support the family. "I don't want to sound like Saint Matthew, but I found out that hard work pays off," he says. After college, Broderick joined the Marines to see what Vietnam was like. He got there in 1969 and came back with a Bronze Star for heroism. As a platoon commander and second lieutenant, the lowest rank for an officer, Broderick organized and led his men in a night counterattack against a North Vietnamese battalion in Quang Tri province, "repeatedly exposing himself to the hostile fusillade," the presidential citation reads. Broderick was twenty-three years old.

Broderick brought back from Vietnam a reputation as a superb military tactician and a quick-tempered brawler. And as a leader whose fierce devotion to his Marines ought not to be challenged. That is why he demands so much of his men: to make certain they know what they are doing when they get to Somalia, to make certain they can operate as a team, and to ensure—as far as possible—that everyone can get back home safely. It means that when the MEU puts into a foreign port for hard-earned liberty, he wants his Marines to party hard.

And it means that if anybody stands in the way of his Marines' welfare, he politely removes that obstacle. Aboard the *Wasp* one day, Broderick learned that someone had barred his Marines from fresh air and exercise on the flight deck. "Goddamn it, you're fuckin' with my Marines!" he bellowed into the phone. Within minutes, the ship's public address system, the 1MC, was blaring: "The flight deck is now open for PT [physical training]!"

The United States Treasury has entrusted Broderick with $3,515,700 to operate the MEU for a year. Every cost comes out of Broderick's accounts. He rents his infantry troops, the vehicles, and the desert camouflage uniforms they were given when the *Wasp* sailed for Somalia. When the MEU gets back in August, a broken or missing piece of gear will be charged to the account. A few months ago, Broderick had to take his men out for field training. He shopped around and found a bargain at Fort A. P. Hill in Virginia, an Army installation. He had to rent buses to get his men there and hire a caterer to bring in hot food.

This system of saddling individual commanders like Broderick with responsibility for their own checkbooks is in keeping with the Marine Corps's ethic of individual accountability. It is not some unseen bureaucracy that handles the money: it is the colonel himself and a handful of young Marines like Chris Roupp and Scott Rogers.

Rogers is an amiable twenty-five-year-old corporal from Amesbury, Mass. He has blond hair, an open, freckled face, and a knack for computers. Rogers is charged with watching Broderick's money. To make it simpler, he has written a new computer program to identify and track expenditures. He works closely with Roupp, a wiry sergeant who grew up in Corning, N.Y.

The MREs that provided Staff Sergeant North his coffee on Purple

Beach tonight were ordered by Roupp. He has figured out the precise number of MREs required, phoned up the supply guys, had the cartons of MREs packaged onto wooden pallets, and arranged for the pallets to be lifted from the hold and loaded onto the boats going ashore. Roupp has ordered ammunition, water, fuel, spare tires, and a thousand other items, choreographing the complicated movement of supplies and Marines and boat or helo transportation like a young maestro.

Rogers tracks each item going out, logs its unit cost, and keeps a running total. Every Friday, Broderick sits down to pore over his accounts. It is not a chore he enjoys.

"The Marine Corps, of course, doesn't give you enough money, so you gotta get creative," he says without offering elaboration.

Most of the time his thoughts and energy are directed toward Somalia.

"Nobody's sharpening his bayonet out here hoping to run it through somebody," he mused one night as the MEU steamed through the Atlantic toward Africa. "These kids are not steely-eyed killers.

"But we're kind of like the fire department. They don't want anybody to get hurt, but yeah, they'd kinda like a fire. We want to demonstrate that America is good and that we can help people. I know that sounds corny, but that's the kind of people we are."

At first glance, all this should look familiar to anyone who's seen a war movie or watched TV news. Indeed, America has sent its young to war since before it was even a country. This black, close air of Purple Beach, laden with dust and smoke and adrenaline, could be Khe Sanh or Normandy, or even the hot predawn hour in the fields around Gettysburg 130 years ago. Except for one thing: unlike those times, these Marines are not the boys next door.

For its major wars, and for peacetime service in the 1950s and 1960s, America drafted hundreds of thousands of civilians and trained them in the basics of war. When their duty was over, in two or three or four years, they poured back into civilian life. The experience defined entire generations. Even those young Americans who never served were intimately connected to those events because they were liable for military duty.

But the abolition of the draft twenty years ago snapped that connection.

During World War II, about eight of ten eligible men were drafted to serve. The Vietnam-era draft, even with its haphazard inequities, brought four in ten eligible males into the military. Today, far less than one in ten American males volunteers to serve in the military. And as the military gets smaller, service becomes even more distant to most Americans. No longer is military service the shared ritual of manhood it was for generations. Today, many Americans don't know a single person in uniform. During the highly popular Persian Gulf war, most mail was addressed to "any soldier."

The military, too, has withdrawn. Burned by its public humiliation in Vietnam twenty-five years ago, it still shuns contact with the press and what it regards as a fickle public. It retreats to enclaves like the Marine Corps base at Camp Lejeune, an oasis of small-town America of the 1960s. Here, the values of honesty, patriotism, morality, and duty are preserved against the corruptions of a society that seems to actively dishonor them.

The result is a dangerously widening chasm between America's military and the society it serves.

Most Americans have no personal stake either in the military or in the distant conflicts to which the military is sent. The shift from conscription to voluntary enlistment—from a system where nearly everyone was liable to be called, to a system where only a few professionals serve—seems to have destroyed the idea of military service as a widely shared obligation of citizenship.

Generations of Americans grow up with no exposure to the military except through television sitcoms, movies, and brief news reports. As a result, the popular image of the military seems to swing wildly between that of a well-oiled and invincible machine (Desert Storm), and a bunch of crude stumblebums (the 1991 Tailhook sexual harrassment scandal).

What's lacking is both an abiding faith in the determination and professionalism of the military, and the keen sense of "GI wisdom" that military service instills: that despite everyone's best efforts, whatever can go wrong probably will go wrong.

People with military experience "sort of instinctively know that everything gets screwed up, that when you're going through an operation, things go wrong," said Brent Scowcroft, a retired Air Force general who served as national security adviser to President Bush.

"Military force is just a very inexact thing," Scowcroft said. "The notion that the population at large has of some scientific application of a certain measure of force that's just right to achieve an objective, without any weapons going wrong, without any friendly fire coming down on our own troops and all that stuff . . . that's just nuts."

Scowcroft spoke somewhat bitterly, for it was against his better judgment that he had helped plan the December 1992 U.S. intervention into Somalia. Scowcroft had deep doubts about the effectiveness of using U.S. combat forces in Somalia, but in the late fall of 1992, the Bush administration had been under intense pressure to do something—anything!—about the starvation in Somalia. The pressure, he said later, was brought by people who knew little about the use of military force.

Most Americans don't understand the imprecision of military operations, he said. "The ignorance is clearly getting worse."

As a result, public discussions about military issues can become grotesque parodies of informed democratic debate. Whether the issue is using American troops to try to halt the slaughter in Bosnia, or the rights of homosexuals to serve openly in the armed services, the debate seems to turn more on emotional exaggeration and caricature than on knowledgeable reason. During the debates in 1993 over using U.S. military forces in Bosnia, much was said and written about America's moral duty to save those in distress. Little was said about the morality of sending young Americans on a poorly defined mission.

And because most of the public has little personal stake in the outcome, such military issues tend to be discussed in airy, hypothetical terms among experts. The public mostly sits it out, offering neither the prowar passions of late 1942 nor the antiwar protests of 1968.

The changed nature of warfare has further widened the distance between mainstream America and its military. No more are conflicts great crusades with the nation's vital interests in peril and a clean victory to be won. Instead, the conflicts of today are messy, murky affairs. Popular villains are rare. These conflicts are risky for those who are sent, and hair-raising for the families they leave behind. Yet they hold no personal claim on most Americans. They are soon forgotten, except by those who were there.

On Purple Beach, the last forlorn notes of "Amazing Grace" die away. The few dozen Marines stand on the beach with their heads bowed. They are praying now, seeking to ease their fatigue and foreboding with ancient words of comfort and faith. Make a joyful noise unto the Lord, all ye lands, for in a few hours we move out. I shall fear no evil, for Thou are with me.

The sounds stir North from beside the dying embers of his fire. "We fear no evil," he mutters, "because we're the meanest damn sons a bitches around."

QUESTION: Why did you choose the Marine Corps rather than another service?

I first thought Air Force, took and passed all the tests. I had a friend that was USMC who was killed in 'Nam. I had some wild idea that I would avenge his death but the war ended two weeks before I got out of boot camp.
—Gunnery Sergeant, Aircraft Technician

The Marines definitely had the best-looking uniforms and seemed a lot tougher and more military. Marine boot camp was longer and tougher-sounding than the Army. That and the fact that my Dad (killed when I was nine months old) had been a Marine.
—Sergeant, Air Traffic Control

2

POLICY TOWN

PURPLE BEACH, SOMALIA, and WASHINGTON, D.C.

March 1993

Moving in five mikes! Let's go, rouse out!"

It is 0400 at Purple Beach. Marines everywhere call it zero-dark thirty, the blackest hour before dawn, the time favored by Marine commanders to launch operations. With the five-minute warning, Staff Sergeant North is fumbling with his poncho liner, a thin quilt on which he has been jerked from four hours of deep sleep, trying to fold it into a package that will fit into his pack. Michael Bowlin is firing up the Hell Bitch's huge diesel engine. Erik Dacey is peeing into the darkness. Marines everywhere are stumbling and grumbling, pulling on flak jackets, checking weapons, filling canteens, shouting and cavorting to burn away the sudden surge of adrenaline.

At this hour, few of them pause to wonder precisely how they got here; it is enough that they are here and have to deal with that reality.

In fact few of them—and not many other Americans—comprehend the process by which American military forces are landed on distant shores like Purple Beach.

From outside Washington's famous Beltway, the business of government sometimes seems incomprehensible. Up close, it looks worse. In the babble of voices, the struggle of competing interests, the clanging din of everyday politics, there is little time for thoughtful, long-range planning.

What often emerges instead is a series of short-term decisions that can acquire the force—and deadly effect—of an avalanche.

Marine, Purple Beach.

Such was the case with the crisis in Somalia.

In 1992, with Somalia barely a blip on the capital's political-warning system, every American family sent to Washington about $2,600 earmarked for safeguarding American interests abroad during the coming year: to help make the world a safe and prosperous place for Americans, and to deal with the consequences when that effort fails.

The money, siphoned out of taxpayers' pockets through payroll deductions and income taxes, amounted to some $320 billion. In the months that followed its arrival in Washington, it was the object of a frenzied struggle among diplomats, generals, senators and congressmen, lobbyists, interest groups, technocrats, and editorial writers.

The arguments on how the money should be spent filter, as they do every year, up and down through layers of government and its attendant colonies of interest groups and opinion-makers who have a say in the making of national security policy and the spending of money to implement the policy.

This is a vast, circular enterprise—untouched by the end of the Cold War and the much-touted downsizing of the national security establishment. It stretches from Washington's Capitol Hill, along the plush offices of lawyers and lobbyists on K Street, to the White House and the block-long main building of the State Department, then jumps across the river to the Pentagon and rolls on out to northern Virginia where the Central Intelligence Agency hums along in its university-like setting and where policy consultants, think tanks, and defense contractors repose in gleaming suburban office buildings linked by limousine and fax to Capitol Hill.

On Capitol Hill, fourteen full committees (and their staffs) have a finger in the money and policy pie, along with forty-two subcommittees (and their staffs). At the Pentagon, where electric carts deliver mail along 17.5 miles of corridors to the building's four Zip Codes, are suites of offices for under secretaries, assistant secretaries, their deputies and their staffs, directorates, commissions, bureaus and agencies and their executive directors, administrative officers, planners, consultants, information management specialists, budgeteers, affirmative action supervisors, and paperwork managers.

In all, some twenty-four thousand people work each day at the Defense Department, a bureaucracy equaled in size, reach, and ornateness of titles ("Executive Director of the Office of the Principal Deputy Assistant Secretary") at the Department of State.

The noise and momentum generated by these officials are amplified and accelerated by the corporate lobbyists, interest groups, and think tanks (the Washington phone book contains 141 entries beginning with "Institute," from the Institute on African Affairs to the Institute on Terrorism and Sub-National Conflict). Together, they produce a blizzard of studies, reports, and recommendations which are solemnly discussed at dozens of symposiums and conferences that clutter Washington's calendar.

The decisions focus money and attention on one or another of the world's potential trouble spots. And because there are bureaucratic winners and losers in these decisions, they are constantly being revised, renegotiated, reversed, or put on hold.

Sudden crises periodically jolt this activity into a new frenzy. Terrorists strike, governments fall, earthquakes erupt, brush-fire wars flare, refugees flee.

A generation ago, these might have been ignored. Now they intrude instantly on television screens in living rooms, congressional offices, think tank suites, newspaper offices, and the action officers' cubbyholes inside the National Military Command Center at the Pentagon. Positions are staked out, congressional hearings and interagency meetings are convened. Speeches are made, op-ed articles written, politicians and experts pontificate on TV talk shows. Action is demanded.

All of this is shoveled by the thousands of journalists accredited to Washington into the insatiable maw of the media and spit out in undigested sound bites and breathless headlines that are as unrelenting as they are meaningless: IRANIAN TROOPS MASS ALONG AZERI BORDER. THATCHER, SHULTZ URGE AIR STRIKES. MILITARY CHIEF FEARS NATO EXPANSION. HOUSE CUTS DEFENSE SPENDING. TOP GENERAL SAYS FUTURE IS "UNCLEAR." MARINES MAY BE SENT TO SOMALIA.

The actors in this ongoing drama are among the smartest and most dedicated men and women the country can offer. Most are drawn to the capital by a sense of civic duty. They come with the ambition to do better than the previous generation.

Sure, there is glamour and money: There are 128 limousine services in the city, and lunch for two at The Prime Rib, one of dozens of packed restaurants among the lobbyists' offices on K Street, goes for over ninety dollars. But most of the people who labor to harness the unwieldy national security establishment to serve the nation's highest goals put in long hours, eat brown-bag lunches, and take their work seriously.

Thus it was perhaps not the people, but the system, that failed the Somalis, and failed the Americans who were sent to help them, and failed the Americans who paid for it and hoped it would work.

It is difficult to imagine a place, a people, and a culture more foreign to Washington than Somalia: a region of vast, sun-baked plains where tribal nomads have for centuries scratched out a precarious existence raising and trading goats, camels, and cattle.

The cutting wind and periodic lashing storms have deeply scored the stony landscape and hardened its tall, proud people of black skins and Arabic blood. Periodic droughts devastate their herds and thin their ranks. Their hardscrabble struggle for existence has spawned a gritty determination to survive and a fierce warrior ethic polished over centuries of cattle raids and territorial wars.

In the imperial land-grab of the late nineteenth century, the Somalis' Texas-size territory was divided up between Britain and Italy, but even after Somalia became an independent country in 1960 it remained mostly a primitive desert society. Until strategists in the Kremlin and the Pentagon realized that Somalia, lying at the gateway to the Red Sea and adjacent to the oil fields of Arabia, was a rich Cold War prize.

First in were the Russians, who replaced the nomads' primitive weapons with automatic rifles, howitzers, rocket-launchers, and tanks. The Russians gave Somalia a few late-1940s MiG fighters, flown by Soviet pilots in ceremonial formations above reviewing stands built for Somali generals and VIPs.

Then, in a series of chessboard moves bewildering to Western newspaper readers and nomads alike, the Russians abandoned Somalia for Ethiopia, Somalia's next-door neighbor, whose new Marxist revolutionary government frowned on Americans. The United States obligingly closed up shop in Ethiopia and reopened in Somalia, which it promptly declared a solid Cold War ally. More important to Washington than Somalia's shifting political loyalties was a half-finished Russian base on the Somali coast. It would soon be designated the jumping-off place for the new U.S. Rapid Deployment Force, formed to defend the Arabian oil fields from Russian invasion.

Somalia at the time was engaged in a sputtering war with Ethiopia. Washington condemned the war and pumped in about one hundred million dollars worth of "defensive" arms, including armored personnel carriers, antitank missiles, artillery, rifles, machine guns, and Huey helicopters.

As the Cold War ended, so did superpower interest in Somalia. The Pentagon never used its thirty-five-million-dollar Rapid Deployment Force base. When war did break out in the Arabian oil fields, U.S. troopers jumped off from North Carolina and flew past Somalia at thirty-three thousand feet.

In a monument of sorts to the fleeting superpower interest in Somalia, a pile of rusting wreckage lies at one end of the Mogadishu airport. At the bottom of the heap are the corroding bodies of Russian MiGs. At the top, the rusting hulks of the American Hueys.

With the superpower "advisers" gone, Somalia reverted back to its traditional clan-based power struggles. But this time, it had all the lethal firepower that Moscow and Washington left behind. No longer were skirmishes fought by untrained nomads with single-shot rifles. This time there was a new generation of young Somalis eager for the prestige of the warrior and the glory of combat—perhaps not smartly uniformed, but trained and equipped with the most deadly personal-combat weapons the world could offer.

The national security establishment in Washington was slow to respond to the developing crisis in Somalia. Hardly anyone in Washington had ever been there. It was too far away. It was too hard to pronounce the names of the various clans and factions. Anyway, no Americans were involved. No strategic U.S. interests, either.

But in the summer of 1992, Congress and the Bush administration, lashed by daily television pictures of starving Somali children, began to stir. Speeches were made. Action was demanded. America had responded before to famines in that part of the world.

From Washington, this looked like another heart-wrenching famine. It wasn't. It was a war.

Somalis live on a meager and precarious food supply, but they do live. There is, barely, enough food to go around. If drought burns the sparse grass off the baked clay flatlands of central Somalia, people move their herds and families south toward the fertile Juba River valley.

This time, though, the Somali armies struggling for ascendancy in what had become a civil war were sweeping through the countryside, killing livestock and burning crops to deny them to the enemy—the African equivalent of U.S. General William Tecumseh Sherman's ruthless 1864 scorched-earth march from Atlanta to the sea.

Thus the problem in Somalia was not nature, but man.

Food supplies shipped into Mogadishu were being ripped off by the Somalia clan soldiers hired as "security guards" by the United Nations and private relief organizations. One gang alone was extorting twenty thousand dollars a week for this "protection."

32

In the midsummer of 1992, a few people in Congress were becoming alarmed by the unfolding of what seemed to be another humanitarian crisis. Just before it adjourned for its August vacation, the House of Representatives passed a resolution urging President Bush to "work with the United Nations Security Council to deploy security guards immediately. . . ."

During a brief floor discussion, Representative William S. Broomfield, Republican of Michigan, thundered, "Our great nation must send . . . an unambiguous message to the world that the U.S. Congress will not sit idly by while such a devastating human rights disaster unfolds before our very eyes."

The House action was not legally binding. It did not mention military forces, let alone U.S. troops. Yet it was the first step toward the commitment of U.S. military force to Somalia. Unremarkable in itself—and virtually unnoticed by television and newspapers—the House action helped to trigger the accumulation of political and public pressure on the Pentagon and the White House that would in the end put the Marines on Purple Beach and sentence more than forty-four American troops to death.

As this first step was taken, not one voice of caution was raised publicly on Capitol Hill.

At the White House that fall of 1992, President Bush was deep in a reelection campaign, the political fight of his life. He was paying little attention to Somalia. The Pentagon wasn't paying attention either; it was focused on the ethnic slaughter in Bosnia. As the nation drifted toward a consensus to do something for Somalia—anything!—only one dissenting voice was demanding attention. Smith Hempstone, Jr., the outspoken U.S. ambassador to Kenya, cabled the State Department warning against the danger of "embracing the Somali tar baby.

"I do not think Somalia is amenable to the quick fix so beloved of Americans," Hempstone told his superiors.

On December 4, 1992, three days after Hempstone sent his cable, Bush announced his decision to send U.S. forces into Somalia "on a mission that can ease suffering and save lives . . ." Within hours, Marines were pouring ashore.

It wasn't for another sixty-three days that Congress got around to considering whether it was a good idea to send young American troops into the bloody maelstrom of Somalia to try to deliver food.

Even then, on February 4, 1993, the Senate only took ten minutes of its time on the issue before voting to approve the action that the now-retired president had taken.

Doubts were raised by only one senator, Republican Slade Gorton of Washington. He identified the problem as not one of food distribution, but rather as one of war. And he questioned whether the twenty-eight thousand troops sent to Somalia would be enough to solve the problem—to disarm the warring Somalia factions and the security guards, and to keep the peace while a political settlement was worked out. Go in to win, he advised, or stay out.

Gorton's reservations were ignored, and the Senate turned to more pressing business: designating April 1993 as Civil War History Month, and voting to remove "Select" from the title of the Select Committee on Indian Affairs.

In the drift toward U.S. military intervention in Somalia, the few voices of caution were drowned out. The vast national security apparatus—unwieldy and untidy, but presumed to contain the checks and balances and voices of wisdom inherent in a democracy—failed to analyze the problem clearly and to design a pragmatic response.

"What was missing was a strategic vision for Somalia, one that could have integrated political goals with the missions assigned to the military," Walter C. Clarke, a senior U.S. Foreign Service officer with years of experience in the region, wrote months later in an essay for *Parameters*, the quarterly journal of the U.S. Army War College.

Once U.S. troops had landed in Mogadishu, the U.S. national security establishment failed once more.

The United States had agreed to undertake the mission in Somalia on behalf of the UN, which has no troops of its own. The UN asked that the clan armies in Somalia be disarmed, as a prelude to political reconciliation. The United States refused. Senior Pentagon officers said privately that it would take many, many more than the twenty-eight thousand U.S. troops in Somalia to forcibly disarm the Somalis. No politician wanted to commit many, many more troops.

So no one disarmed the warlords. Military commanders and diplomats in Somalia were left to struggle with the problem on their own. As a result, some troops were directed to confiscate certain weapons from individual Somalis while other troops ignored armed Somalis. The warlords' arsenals were left alone.

Months later Brent Scowcroft, Bush's national security adviser, acknowledged that this had been "a major error.

"We assumed that we could turn the problem over to the UN as a political problem," he said. The White House and the Pentagon, he added, were terrified of getting "bogged down" in combat in Somalia.

So why were military troops sent at all? Pressure from the public and the media, Scowcroft said, asserting that the pressure "was absolutely tremendous."

None of this explanation is useful right now, in March of 1993, to the crew of the fifteen-ton armored vehicle known as the Hell Bitch.

Staff Sergeant Mortimer is sitting in the commander's hatch as the convoy rumbles out into the dusty countryside. Perched behind him, sweating heavily in the sweltering humidity of the Somali dawn, are North and Flores and a half-dozen other Marines, swathed against the dust in flak jackets and helmets and goggles and scarves. They sit cross-legged, back to back, scanning the scrub and thorn trees passing by under their rifle barrels.

Suddenly, one of the Hell Bitch's eight huge tires blows out on the rocky path. Mortimer climbs out and soon discovers that the Hell Bitch's jack is broken. He throws his helmet disgustedly on the ground.

"Well, fuck me to tears, what the hell else is gonna go wrong?"

Marines/military people are not closed-minded, ultraconservative right-wing Republicans. Most of us are "middle of the road" and are more open-minded than many of the so-called liberals. . . . Also, politicians—I hate it when rich, spoiled, conceited, and arrogant politicians preach about the need for sacrifice. Hypocrites! Finally, I believe Elvis is alive!
—Captain, Infantry

Many civilians don't get paid the money that they deserve, just like in the military. The teachers in our country don't get squat for doing one of the most important jobs this country needs to have done. The people who mean the most to the greatness of our country get the shit pay and the people who sit on their asses, being hard asses, get all the money.
—Navy Corpsman

3

HELL BITCH
SOUTHERN SOMALIA
March 1993

It takes the crew of the Hell Bitch twenty minutes to change the tire.

Mortimer and Flores and Bowlin borrow a jack from another vehicle, wrestle a spare down off the vehicle's roof eight feet above the ground, and heave the flat back up. North stands guard with Jeffrey Beegle, a twenty-three-year-old rifleman from Holidaysburg, Pa, and with Carl Chapman. A lean-faced former drill sergeant, Chapman is twenty-four. His gravelly parade-ground voice still retains the nasal twang of his native Salisbury, Mass. He has the habit of punctuating his dour pronouncements on life with a drawn-out "shee-it."

Now they're rolling again, sipping from water bottles and watching the scenery pass. It is just past six in the morning, but already the air is sticky and hot. The dull gnawings of fear evident last night at Purple Beach evaporate in the heat and dust kicked up by the long convoy.

North and Chapman, riding atop the Hell Bitch, warily eye a small settlement that emerges through the dust. Chest-high huts, built of sticks plastered with mud and pieces of cardboard, lean against each other. Scrawny goats nose at the edges of cooking fires. A few men watch stone-faced as the column rumbles past. A child wearing a pair of ragged, over-size shorts waves shyly. North rewards him with a huge smile and a salute.

"Cowabunga, Julio," he shouts.

"Pitiful," he adds, as if the rags and the dismal huts were the child's own fault.

Chapman squirts a stream of tobacco juice over the side. "People

Moving out, dawn.

back home oughta see this," he growls. "They'd stop complaining and think about what they have." He spits again. "Shee-it."

The Hell Bitch bounces and lurches along, one of thirty-nine armored vehicles headed one hundred forty miles deep into the southern Somalia interior. Every few minutes, a pair of dull gray Harrier jets streaks along either side of the convoy, skimming the tawny scrubland at two hundred feet. At a further distance, two Cobra helicopter gunships keep pace with the column.

Broderick and his 2,100 Marines have been in Somalia for about a week. Their precise mission is unclear. Most of the twenty-eight thousand U.S. troops sent to help feed starving Somalis in December 1992, four months ago, have been sent home. Most Somalis are getting food. Most of the international media in Somalia have gone home, too, having sent final stories about the success of the U.S. and UN intervention in Somalia.

But the underlying tensions that ignited Somalia's civil war remain unabated. The warlords, under UN pressure, have stacked most of their weapons in caches. The UN command in Mogadishu is cautiously taking over from American military commanders the job of coordinating the delicate military and political and diplomatic efforts of peacemaking. The

Hell Bitch.

UN has begged Washington to have U.S. troops disarm the warlords. Washington, fearing a Vietnam-like quagmire, stubbornly refuses. But as it withdraws most of its troops, Washington offers the 24th MEU to the UN command in Mogadishu as "insurance" in case things get sticky.

As the *Wasp* dropped anchor off Mogadishu, its officers choppered ashore to confer with the UN. There, another reason for their presence became clear. Several of the European nations who have sent peacekeeping troops here are uneasy with the United States pulling out. If all-out war reignites, they want to know that the United States will return. The 24th MEU is that insurance.

"We are the bait to keep the other countries here," said one officer.

Broderick attacked this confusing situation with his customary zeal. He is not a patient man. He strides through life as if he is wading through surf, leaning forward with his arms and legs pumping vigorously.

He waded into UN headquarters in Mogadishu scarcely bothering to introduce himself.

"We do windows," he barked at the startled UN generals. "We'll do anything. Tell us what you need done."

He was told, in effect, to go down to southern Somalia, look around, and see what needs to be done. Broderick choppered back to *Wasp* and started to figure out how to apply his Marines' skills to the treacherous situation in Somalia.

On the conference table in his tiny office aboard the *Wasp*, Broderick spread out maps and overhead photos taken by his Harriers on a reconnaissance flight. His attention was drawn to southern Somalia, specifically to Kismayu, the sprawling coastal city that is second in size only to Mogadishu. For weeks, Mogadishu had been quiet. It was, after all, intensively patrolled by the Marines sent there in December. It was so safe that Sophia Loren and Charlton Heston and boxer Riddick Bowe had come to visit.

Kismayu, two hundred eighty miles to the south, was another story. The city was occupied by a few hundred Belgian paratroopers. That wasn't enough. Two weeks before Broderick and his men arrived, a local warlord named Mohammed Said Hirsi infiltrated three hundred of his fighters into the city's narrow, crooked streets and in a fierce battle, ousted the local clan army run by rival warlord Omar Jess.

Under threat of immediate attack by U.S. troops, Hirsi had withdrawn his men to his stronghold in a village named Doobhley, deep in the Somalia interior. Jess and his men were allowed to come home to Kismayu. But U.S. and UN commanders in Mogadishu were concerned that the violence would spread from Kismayu and plunge the country back into war.

Broderick was trying to determine how that might be prevented. Washington had given him no authority to disarm the warlords and not enough men and firepower to subdue them, the two obvious military strategies. In fact, under the compromise rules drawn up by U.S. and UN commanders in Mogadishu, each warlord was allowed to have huge arms caches, or storage bunkers, that the Marines were not allowed to inspect.

Above all, Washington had told its military commanders not to get bogged down in combat. This is, after all, only a humanitarian mission. No "decisive engagement."

Given these restrictions, Broderick tried the only remaining alternatives. He landed a heavily armed force ashore at Kismayu, along a section of the coastline the Marines designated as Purple Beach. About two hundred Marines were detailed to help the Belgians keep order in the city. Broderick put out reconnaissance teams to monitor the flow of weapons and people.

And he ordered the armored convoy to speed all the way to Hirsi's

North and villagers.

stronghold in Doobhley. There, it was planned that the Marines would burst out of the dawn and impress upon Hirsi that if he caused trouble again, he'd have to deal with United States Marines.

"We're not looking for a fight," Broderick told a CNN camera crew on board the *Wasp* the day before the convoy was launched. "We're the town cops, walking the beat, shaking hands and meeting people." To his officers, Broderick offered a slightly different view. "If anybody moves," he growled, referring to the warlords and their fighters, "we're gonna be right in his face."

Now, twenty-four hours later, the Hell Bitch and the rest of the convoy snakes through the narrow streets of Kismayu. The Marines are

tense; their weapons are locked and loaded. All of them have signed life insurance papers choosing either a lump-sum or annual payments to their next of kin. Many have written last letters home. There are bad guys out there with guns. This is real.

"Well Come," says a neat hand-lettered sign on a heavily mildewed one-story cement building.

"Peace is the Key of Live," says another slogan painted on a crumbling building whose original coat of pastel pink and green paint is covered with decades of grime and mildew. Along the roadside, women swathed in bright gauzy material sell sweet tea and Sportsman cigarettes from rickety tables. The air is redolent with dust and the smoke of cooking fires.

Flocks of children run alongside the huge vehicles, grinning and laughing and saluting. After a while the Marines start waving back. This is turning out to be less like D-Day and more like the liberation of Paris.

"Hey, 'Merigo!" shouts a young boy.

"Marine," North shouts back. "Mah-reen. Mah . . . *reen!*"

"Mah-*reen*," the boy yells delightedly. North waves back.

On rolls the convoy, enveloped in a thick cloud of its own dust and diesel fumes. The rear hatches of the Hell Bitch are open, its cargo compartment crammed with jerry cans of fuel and water, spare parts, toolboxes, cartons of MREs, spare ammunition, personal packs, canteens, and medical supplies.

Each Marine has lugged along two packs. One is a backpack, or ALICE (All-purpose Lightweight Individual Carrying Equipment) pack, which is supposed to contain a poncho with liner, T-shirt, underwear, towel, facecloth, foot powder, soap, razor, toothbrush, mirror, weapons cleaning gear, mosquito head-net, running shorts, goggles, socks, shower sandals, wet-weather jacket, flashlight, and malaria pills.

The other is a butt pack, holding an MRE, extra socks, a couple of packets of powdered fruit drink, Chapstick, earplugs (to be worn in helos), sunglasses, and gloves.

Aside from this stuff, each Marine is wearing his web or "deuce" gear, consisting of a broad web belt with webbed shoulder straps that act as suspenders. Each man wears on his deuce gear two canteens, a first aid kit, ammo pouches, and assorted other gear which might include a compass, a sheathed knife, a pair of gloves attached with a carabiner, and, on the shoulder belts, a flashlight and notebook pouch. Senior NCOs and officers wear a 9-mm semiautomatic pistol.

In addition, each Marine has put on olive-drab shorts and T-shirt, heavy cotton desert camouflage utilities, heavy black boots, a thick flak vest, a heavy Kevlar helmet, and a gauzy olive-drab scarf.

Finally, of course, each man has at least one weapon, usually the 8.8-pound M16 rifle. Many Marines carry the lightweight machine gun called a SAW, or Squad Automatic Weapon. It fires five hundred rounds a minute and weighs twenty pounds. At least one man in each platoon carries a radio. The age of electronic miniaturization has not reached the Marine Corps; its field radio, the PRC-77, is essentially what Marines carried on their backs in Vietnam. It weighs about as much as a ten-year-old child.

Strapping all this on is something like putting on an overcoat that has a dozen concrete blocks sewn into the lining. Combat-loaded Marines leave deep footprints and they are known, with reason, as "grunts." Marine reconnaissance scouts working in marshy areas at night routinely stow their ALICE pack gear in airtight bags, hoping that when they fall into deep pools of water, they will float. (Sometimes they do.)

The Marines riding on the Hell Bitch have little to be thankful for, but they are thankful for this: They are riding and not walking. Their packs are thrown in the back of the Hell Bitch along with everything else, and what with Mortimer looking for the jack and toolbox and people rummaging around for MREs, things have gotten pretty stirred up.

"Somebody ratfucked my shit," mutters Chapman, trying to unearth his canteen.

Chapman and North and Flores and Daryl Kyllonen, a twenty-three-year-old Navy corpsman, bounce along in suffocating silence. Like farm-workers on the back of a pickup truck, they perch on the edge of the open hatch doors, lashed by occasional thorn tree branches and whipped by

Flores (left), Kyllonen.

the dusty wind. When that gets too uncomfortable, they slide down and curl up in the cargo bay, where there is some shade but not a breath of air. In either position it is stiflingly hot, cramped, and dusty.

The Marines are under strict orders from the MEU's medical officers to suck down water. A quart and a half every hour is supposed to reduce the risk of heat exhaustion. Even with a raging thirst, it's hard to get that much of the warm, tinny-tasting stuff down. (Aside from the dangers of heat, the Marines have been warned of mosquitos and ticks carrying malaria, break-bone fever, yellow fever, Baghdad sore, typhus, plague, and Congo hemorrhagic fever. They have been warned of poisonous spiders and tarantulas, scorpions, and snakes, including spitting cobras, puff adders, mambas, vipers, and boomslangs. The dust itself, now caking on the Marines' faces and arms, contains hookworms, roundworms, and whipworms which cause red snakelike trails under the skin.)

Far ahead in the lead vehicle is Dion Condry, a lanky nineteen-year-old from Jefferson, Ga. He calls the convoy to a clanking halt in order to stop to search a broken-down truck being hauled toward the convoy by a tractor. An ancient rifle is confiscated from the four Somali men riding in the truck. They protest, saying the rifle is for hunting; as evidence, they point to a freshly killed gazelle tied to the rear of the truck.

Condry feels bad, but he has orders. In return for the rifle, he hands the men four twenty-five-pound sacks of wheat. Later he says, "I saw one of the bags ripped open and left there with wheat spilling out of it. It looked like animals had gotten into it."

The sun sinks toward the west and the convoy rumbles on. The Marines sag with fatigue. Chapman reaches for an MRE, slices it open with his knife: the universally hated chicken à la king. He sloshes it with the tiny bottle of Tabasco sauce provided in the package. He rips the plastic wrapper off the plastic spoon and stirs the mess dejectedly. It is coated with light brown dust. He spoons it into his dry mouth, grimaces, and washes it down with a swig of warm canteen water.

"Want a cold beer?" someone asks. Chapman barks a laugh. "Shee-it."

Now it is well after midnight and the convoy rumbles on. Down in his cramped driver's compartment, Bowlin blinks repeatedly to keep his eyes open and on the road. Up top, Flores and Beegle doze, sitting back to back, their heads lolling on each other's shoulders. North is slumped on MRE cartons in the cargo bay, his legs lying across Chapman's legs.

Chapman (left), North.

Kyllonen's head rests on North's chest. Their fatigues are soaked with sweat and layered with dust. The dust cakes around their lips and gums their eyes.

In their own miserable way, the Marines like what they're doing. This is hard stuff, and they can take it.

During a short pause, they leap off the Hell Bitch and without a word set up a perimeter guard, rifles pointed out into the blackness.

Up ahead, the convoy commander is trying to establish communications with Broderick aboard the *Wasp*.

No go.

Like much of the Marines' gear, the satellite phone is old and unreliable. In Washington, lobbyists commonly outfit their limousines with cellular telephones and fax machines. It's part of the (tax-deductible) cost of doing government business. Out here, as the saying goes, Marines make do with hand-me-down gear made years ago by the lowest bidder. It's part of the cost of serving the government.

Hell Bitch crew: (standing, from left) Donald Mortimer, Jon Flores, Michael Bowlin, Norman North, Army PFC David Culp, Daryl Kyllonen; (kneeling, from left) Carl Chapman, Jeffrey Beegle.

Soon, a message crackles along the line of vehicles: "Moving out!" The Marines heave themselves aboard their vehicles and roll off.

There are compensations.

One is their physical closeness. On a crowded subway back in the civilian world, these men would shrink from having their knee touch a seatmate's thigh. Here, those inhibitions are absent. Exhausted, lonely, a bit concerned that their entry into Doobhley might be contested by Somali gunmen, they welcome the touch of another human being. In the cramped cargo space of the Hell Bitch, it is necessary. It is also comforting.

Marines say this is something few civilians can understand. It is an important part of their resistance to having openly gay Marines in their ranks. In the stress of combat operations, Major Mike Dick explains, "somebody puts his hand on your shoulder and it's tremendously comforting, reassuring. To throw a sexual aspect in there, whether it's women Marines or gays, it just screws with that formula."

Emotional closeness is another compensation. When Marines are miserable, and that is much of the time, they are miserable together—captains, privates, sergeants, and lance corporals. This is true even at boot camp, whose central fact of life is the unbridgeable social chasm between "boots" and drill instructors (DIs). Chapman fondly recalls those days, when DIs made life miserable for the young boots, and everyone hated everyone else so bad that the lust for revenge was the only thing motivating them through boot camp.

"And there would come a time when you'd 'fall out' a formation and dismiss 'em for the last time, and there'd be a tear in your eye," Chapman growls. "A lotta DIs try to act hard and deny it, but these boots are like your family, like your little brothers. . . . Shee-it."

Zero-dark thirty, 4 A.M. civilian time. The convoy is stopped on the road outside Doobhley. Marines are roused from their cramped positions in the cargo bay and from the poncho liners spread on the dirt where they have caught almost three hours sleep. With muffled shouts and curses, the column growls into life. Headlights blink on, men leap onto vehicles, weapons at the ready.

In the gray dawn, the column prowls into town. If the warlord and his fighters are cowering here, there is no evidence: Aside from a few women staggering along under bundles of firewood and buckets of water, the town of a few dozen humble buildings seems deserted. As the convoy pauses on the outskirts of town to regroup, a mourning dove alights in a tree and watches with round eyes.

Ahead—back the way the convoy has come—lie 180 miles of dusty, rutted trails leading to Purple Beach, where the Marines will hose down their vehicles, load onto landing craft, and—tomorrow, if all goes well—head back to the *Wasp* for hot showers, hot chow, and real beds.

It is another twenty-one-hour day. The Marines are in the peak of physical condition, but among the three hundred of them in the convoy, a half dozen fall from heat exhaustion. Two serious cases are medevaced back to the *Wasp* by helo; because the road is too narrow for a helo to land, two vehicles plunge into the thorn thickets and trample down a hasty landing zone barely big enough to accommodate the helo's whirling blades.

On the Hell Bitch in early afternoon, North notices that Kyllonen, a quiet kid from Michigan with a soft brown crew cut, has been too quiet. Under questioning, Kyllonen admits that he is nauseated and dizzy, can't keep down water. His forehead is burning. Classic heat exhaustion. North heaves the gear around in the cargo bay, making room for Kyllonen to stretch out. He heaves up a five-gallon jerry can of water and pours the entire contents over Kyllonen.

Dawn, outskirts of Doobhley.

For the rest of this long day, North keeps a wary eye on the corpsman, keeping him as comfortable as possible and periodically feeling his forehead and dousing him with water.

North affects the cocky and often crude demeanor common among veteran Marines. But like most of them, he is a more complicated person. He grew up in Carbondale, southern Illinois, the son of a Marine grunt who was badly wounded and blinded at Bougainville in the South Pacific in World War II.

North spent his late teenage years in the Age of Aquarius, when long hair, drugs, and rebellion were in vogue. He did some things he's not particularly proud of now. And some things he is proud of: He spent a few years caring for terminally disabled patients, feeding and bathing them and emptying their bedpans. But he also skirted trouble with the law.

Before it was too late, he straightened himself out and enlisted. He struggled through boot camp five or six years older than the other recruits. In the intervening years he has acquired steady promotions and a kind of jive-ass approach to life. One night aboard the *Wasp*, North put up notices around the ship saying that if Marines are having sex problems with their wives or are getting paid late or have any other complaints, call the number listed below. For days afterward, North's buddies in the *Wasp*'s closed-circuit TV studio were bombarded with telephone calls. "I'm just fuckin' with 'em," North said with a satisfied chuckle.

Just before the MEU left home two months ago, North reenlisted. Broderick swore him in. They both got teary-eyed.

"I'm going off for six months, my daughter was born on my last float and she's gonna grow up not knowing who the hell I am, while I'm floating off some goddamn broke-dick country, leaving my wife to deal with a pay system that always gets screwed up and all the thousand and one other things a wife has to deal with, and why?"

North leans forward with intense eyes.

"Because I love my country, and because it has to be done."

Bouncing along in a vehicle far ahead of the Hell Bitch, Sergeant Major Curtis R. Roderick is thinking the same thing. A twenty-seven-year veteran, Roderick is one of the two most senior NCOs in the MEU. He wears size fifty-two jackets and weighs in at 225. He is used to being listened to.

Roderick has responsibility for all the MEU's enlisted grunts. He regards them with fatherly affection. He served two tours in Vietnam. "That's why I get on these kids in a heartbeat," he said once. "Get your flak [jacket] on, suck down two quarts of water an hour minimum. I don't wanna see them make the same mistake I did, sitting outside during a mortar attack saying, 'This shit don't bother me.'"

Now, Roderick is pondering why these kids make such good Marines, why they perform so well under trying conditions, why they do it at all.

"It's a sense of values," he says finally. "It's compassion for human life. . . . I am a warrior, but not a killer. I believe in the people who are with me here, because they are here doing the right thing."

Roderick sighs heavily. Articulating philosophy doesn't come easy.

"We are going to come to other places where we're not going to know why we're there, but we will understand twenty years down the road. . . . There will be a baby born that might not have been born if we hadn't been out doing our jobs, and that baby will be a good person, a good part of mankind. And it happened because we believed.

"And to have been a part of that," Roderick says, "makes me feel pretty damn good."

Back in the Hell Bitch, North is sponging off Kyllonen's forehead in the jouncing cargo bay just as another emergency arises.

The roar of the diesel engine dies away and the vehicle rolls to a stop. Staff Sergeant Mortimer climbs down into the engine compartment and emerges to announce that the fuel-water separator has failed. Kyllonen painfully moves his legs as Flores rummages in the cargo bay for tools and a spare separator. Flores offers to put it in.

"I can do it," insists Mortimer, disappearing back into the engine compartment.

Flores, who is two full ranks lower than Mortimer, says with a grin, "Watch this, I bet he can't do it."

After ten minutes of cursing, Mortimer emerges, red-faced with rage and frustration. Flores flashes a merry smirk to the crowd in the back of the Hell Bitch. In three minutes, Flores has the new part installed. The Hell Bitch fires up and rolls on.

Midnight, Purple Beach. Kyllonen lies on the sand with an IV in his arm. Still nauseous, he is getting rehydrated intravenously. Mortimer and Flores are sitting cross-legged a few yards away, counting bullets as they repack them by flashlight. Every single round drawn by the Marines before the Doobhley operation must be returned and accounted for. North heats battery-acid coffee on a fire. Beegle and Bowlin, the driver, are out cold.

"Yo, Devil Dogs, rouse out! Cold soda!"

The announcement creates a stampede toward a Marine truck that has just pulled in. It carries two shiny aluminum coffins full of iced sodas. Marines on the truck hand pairs to outstretched hands.

Out on the *Wasp* earlier this day, Chris Roupp and Scott Rogers had been sitting around, wondering what they could do for their buddies out on the convoy. They scrounged up six hundred cans of soda, "borrowed" the coffins, coralled a helo, lugged the sodas up to the flight deck, and got the stuff ashore.

"Piece a cake," Roupp later beams modestly.

Out on the beach, though, the Marines take the soda as their just due.

"Hey, these aren't really cold," somebody complains. One of Roupp's men straightens up on the back of the truck.

"Ah, fuck you," he yells good-naturedly.

Early the next morning the Marines are loading the Hell Bitch and the other vehicles onto landing craft. The *Wasp* waits two miles offshore. Mortimer walks backward across the sand, signaling as Bowlin guides the Hell Bitch over the beach and up the ramp.

Mortimer nearly collides with a paunchy man standing in front of

S Sgt Donald Mortimer, Hell Bitch Commander

the landing craft. The man is a Belgian soldier, apparently assigned to beach duty. His beer belly hangs over a pair of tight swimming briefs. He is baked well-done from long days in the sun. Mortimer is pale and filthy, except where he has washed his face and shaved this morning. He is still wearing his sweat-soaked fatigues, helmet, and flak jacket.

The Belgian poses manfully in front of the Hell Bitch while another Belgian snaps his picture.

"How ya doin'," Mortimer says as he trudges past.

QUESTION: Should women be allowed to compete with men on an equal basis for any assignment within the Marine Corps?

No. Men in the field are crude, mean, and nasty! Where would a woman fit in?
—Corporal, Antitank Missiles

As long as they can carry their load.
—Staff Sergeant, Communications

[Women] are mentally, physically, and emotionally unstable.
—Corporal, Combat Engineers

QUESTION: Should people who are openly gay or declared gay be allowed to serve in the military?

No. All the arguments have been heard before but I guess my reason is the thought of fags in my platoon just makes me want to puke.
—First Lieutenant, Infantry

Yes. The gays are not the problem, it's the society we have that won't accept them. They are already in, they shouldn't have to hide what they are. We should accept them.
—Lance Corporal, Antitank Missiles

No. I live by the Bible and gay people are destined to Hell.
—Staff Sergeant, Infantry

Gays have been in the military as long as there has been a military. As long as they don't hinder the performance of the mission, I think they should be left alone.
—Corporal

Yes. People shouldn't be discriminated [against] on sexual preference. At work you are supposed to be a professional. What you do at home or in private is your own business as long as no one gets hurt.
—Lance Corporal, Aircraft Maintenance

I don't want some fag-bag putting up posters of naked men.
—Lance Corporal, Mortars

4

COMBAT TOWN
CAMP LEJEUNE, NORTH CAROLINA

December 1992

From the modest airport at Jacksonville, N.C., the road to the head-quarters of the 24th MEU at Camp Lejeune winds through stands of lob-lolly pine and then along a four-lane highway that speeds past two forlorn adult-entertainment bars, the Playpen and the Dollhouse ("All Girl Staff").

From the Dollhouse, the road explodes into a riot of fast-food fran-chises along Marine Boulevard (Arby's, Bojangle's, Burger King, Dairy Queen, Domino's, three Hardees, Shoney's, Kentucky Fried Chicken, Lit-tle Caesar's, four McDonald's, two Pizza Huts, two Taco Bells, Wendy's, and seven Subways), wedged among tattoo parlors, furniture rental stores, pawn shops, Saigon Sam's military surplus stores, used-car lots and military-rate motels.

Southeast of town, two lanes of traffic curve off to the right, sweep-ing abruptly out of the jangle and clangor of Jacksonville into a vast peace-ful forest with broad expanses of neatly cropped grass on either side of the parkway. Here, traffic slows and halts for a check and a snappy salute from Camp Lejeune's Marine Corps police.

From that point on, Marines and their families are in a different world. More than one hundred thousand Marines and family members live and work here. Most of the Marines belong to the 2nd Division and its supporting units; there are also schools here for infantry and combat engineers and hospital corpsmen, plus all the rifle ranges, barracks, tank maneuver areas, vehicle storage facilities, ammo bunkers, and chow halls associated with large military forces.

Lejeune is far more than a physical home to Marines. It is their com-

CH-47s slant into Camp Lejeune.

munity, the fullest expression of their sense of moral and spiritual order, a fortress preserved and protected against "the outside."

Traffic moves at the posted twenty-five miles per hour. "Sir" and "Ma'am" are common forms of address. Kids ride bikes to school and postmen stop to chat with housewives in neat subdivisions where each house bears a sign announcing the husband's name and rank.

"It's sort of like the Twilight Zone," says one Marine wife.

In one aspect only does Lejeune differ from the 1960s: Its black residents, who number about one out of five, are thoroughly integrated into the community's rigid social structure. Majors, black and white, live in majors' houses, neat two-story frame houses in neighborhoods of spacious lawns and tall shade trees. Sergeants live in sergeants' neighborhoods, where the houses are attached and the yards are smaller. Single Marines occupy three-story barracks of red brick and assemble for morning formation on adjacent parade grounds.

This town has its own thriving Boy Scout troops and archery clubs, riding stables, convenience stores, police and fire departments, gas stations, movie theaters, hospital, youth clubs boasting skateboard parks and Nintendo, and a shopping mall with supermarket and department store.

Lejeune has its own weekly newspaper, its own bank, liquor store, hotel, and car-rental agency. For vacations, there is little reason to wander beyond Lejeune's sprawling 151,000 acres, which is a little larger than Chicago. Lejeune has its own beach resort on its fourteen miles of Atlantic Ocean beachfront.

It has its own way of telling time (thirteen hundred follows noon on the twenty-four-hour clock), its own holidays (the Marine Corps birthday, November 10). It has its own school system and a sprawling, modern day-care center.

It has chapels and a worship schedule in which Catholic, Protestant, Jewish, and Muslim services are offered everywhere, including Lejeune's prison.

The town has its own language, one that reflects the Marines' tradition and vocation of living aboard ships. Thus a floor is a "deck," a wall a "bulkhead," a doorway a "hatch." ("Sir, the colonel's office is on the second deck, third hatch to starboard, but he won't be back until about thirteen hundred.") Even civilians in Jacksonville will say they have friends who live "aboard" Camp Lejeune.

Life aboard Camp Lejeune revolves around the old, wholesome virtues—early rising and hard work, physical fitness and team sports, two-parent families, responsibility to the community. Duty, honor, and order. It is a demanding yet rewarding life.

"I got out of the Corps to go back to school," says Kevin Blaske, a staff sergeant in the 24th MEU. "In the Marines I had been somebody. I'd been in charge of 120 Marines and eight helos and had done an assault demonstration for the top brass," he says proudly.

"Out there in the quote real world unquote, I was Joe Blow civilian.

I went in to sign up for classes and got in the wrong line. This old lady started yelling at me. I realized to her, I was a nobody. I was a nothing.

"I came back in fast." Blaske grins.

Some newcomers have trouble adapting, of course. The transition from boisterous teenager to professional Marine is not an easy one. Inevitably, bad apples are recruited. In the ten-month period roughly corresponding to the time the 24th MEU is training and deployed, Lejeune police recorded 18 rapes, 53 sexual assaults, 146 simple assaults, and 45 aggravated assaults (with a weapon). The MPs also logged in 618 cases of drunk driving.

For Lejeune's one hundred thousand resident Marines and sailors and their families, that is about average, a significantly lower crime rate than for the nation as a whole (nationwide during 1992, the Justice Department recorded 42.8 rapes and 441.8 aggravated assaults per 100,000 population).

For the offenders, Lejeune, along with the rest of America's military, has its own separate legal system, one vastly different from civilian law.

For instance, it holds that disrespect is a punishable offense. It allows such punishment as imprisonment on rations of bread and water, "hard labor," and the ultimate sanction—dishonorable banishment from the Marines Corps community.

To many civilians, these values and sanctions may seem like fading memories of a bygone era. To Marines, they embody the American way of life.

"The old, traditional values—sure, they still exist," says Willie Porter, a thirty-seven-year-old gunnery sergeant from North Philadelphia. But on the outside, he adds, the view is, "These values don't buy cars, clothes, or pay bills. They don't mean as much any more.

"I don't believe our social values—respect for property, human values—are as honored as when I was going to school," says Porter, a muscular man with a thin mustache and an engaging smile.

"They did away with school prayer, the national anthem, those kinds of things that instill the American spirit as we once knew it. There's very little community; it used to be that people would get together after work, you could trust your neighbor. No more."

As a result, Porter—like many Marines—has simply dropped out of the mainstream of American life. He lives here at Lejeune; his wife, a former sailor, works at the post office, and their daughter, five-year-old Erica, attends Lejeune schools.

Willie Porter.

Porter's disdain for civilian society explains why he puts up with the rigid structure and conformity of Marine Corps life. It also explains why on this day in December 1992 he is preparing for his fourth six-month "float" with the 24th MEU. For even more than at Camp Lejuene, the old values are distilled into a pure essence in the floating pressure cooker of an MEU. Many Marines volunteer again and again for sea duty, knowing they can never truly return to civilian life.

On the outside, Porter says, "They've changed the music and people have changed the way they dance. So I'll listen to the music. But I won't dance."

What drives Lejeune's values, of course, is the mission, and in December of 1992 the mission of the twenty-one hundred Marines of the 24th MEU is to prepare for Somalia.

Or more precisely, since its orders haven't officially come down yet, to prepare for the unknown. For out beyond the neat, well-ordered confines of Camp Lejeune, chaos is making a mockery of the New World Order. Whether its destination will be Somalia or Bosnia or Haiti or some yet-to-erupt crisis, the 24th MEU will sally forth from its fortress here prepared to do anything and to do it quickly.

Matthew Broderick, the MEU commander, set the tone of the mission months ago when his senior staff first assembled to begin their six months of training before deploying out into the world.

One of Broderick's officers later recalled the colonel as saying, "This is the big leagues. This is for real. If you fuck up you're gonna get Marines killed, and I'm gonna leave you out there."

On this gray, wintry morning, they are in rehearsal, in a fast-paced war game called a MEU-EX (Marine Expeditionary Unit Exercise). It is the first time that all the elements of the MEU—infantry, artillery, helicopters, battle staff, intelligence, and logistics—are working together as a team.

Marines define their lives by exercises. In the weeks ahead, Broderick will lead his men through a SOC-EX (Special Operations Capable Exercise) and a TRU-EX (Training in an Urban Environment Exercise) in which Broderick's special commando teams will assault targets in Mobile, Ala.

Exercises are designed to train and test Marines' skills for war. Often they are intended to put so much stress on Marines that people make mistakes, equipment breaks down, things go wrong. Men discover their weak points and correct them. These occasions are known by Marines as leap-

Fast Attack Vehicle crew, Camp Lejeune. From left, Brad Myers, Norman Harris, Tadd "Doc" Woolsey, Michael Rosenberger, Ron Tino.

exes ("Things get so bad you gotta leap through your asshole to get it done," says a Marine).

A bad leap-ex can degenerate into a jerk-ex. That's when higher authorities start out with an unclear idea of what they intend to do. When the unforeseen strikes, they fumble, sending out orders and then countermanding them, assigning units to a task and then changing the assignment, jerking Marines back and forth.

The suffix -ex, from *exercise*, can be usefully attached to other words to make a cynical comment. Shmoozing, for example, is what Marines do when they get together—chat. A shmooze-ex, though, is an organized discussion, usually involving officers, and usually a waste of time.

When high-ranking officers gather formally, for purposes of having

Radio Battalion commandos. From left, Mark Wilmot, Pat Cotter,
Bob Clyatt, Paul Bould.

their pictures taken or meeting with foreign dignitaries, Marines call it a
grip 'n' grin–ex.

This is no grip 'n' grin–ex.

Colonel Broderick has been handed a scenario. It tells him that out
there in the capital of a fictional country, trouble is brewing. Rebel forces
are closing on the city, anti-American sentiment is rising, mobs are in the
streets, the local security forces are probably unwilling or unable to protect American diplomats and businessmen and tourists, and the U.S.
ambassador has asked the Marines to stand by to help.

The scenario may be a little contrived. Everything else is real, including the tension. Broderick's men say they can gauge his mood by the color
of his neck. Right now, Broderick's thick neck is fire-engine red. He and

his men have six hours to plan a straightforward but complex operation involving real people, real helicopters, real chances for screwups.

A rifle company, about two hundred men, will do the mission. They will establish a defensive perimeter in the city to keep the mobs at bay. Some Marines will be detailed to seize and hold key sites, others to take up positions as antisniper teams. The ground-force commander will coordinate with the U.S. ambassador and will attempt to find and secure the cooperation of the city's mayor. Marine teams will collect the Americans to be evacuated, provide them with food, water, and medical treatment if needed, load them on helos, methodically shrink their perimeter, and board the last helo out.

It will be done fast, efficiently, and safely.

What makes this difficult is the number of things that can go wrong. Marines operate under Murphy's Law: Anything that can go wrong, will. Helos break down, the weather shifts and boats can't be launched, radio networks go awry and communications is lost, intelligence proves faulty. People make mistakes.

To foil Murphy, the Marines have devised a "playbook" for each of

Broderick.

the twenty-two operations they are likely to have to do in a hurry. Evacuating civilians is one of them. The others include seizing an airfield, intercepting and taking over ships, urban warfare, hostage rescue, civic action, amphibious raids, and handling mass civilian casualties.

Each of these operations involves a different mix of specialists, equipment, and transportation. Each requires speed and precision in planning and carrying out the mission. To achieve that, each operation is planned, tailored to local conditions, rehearsed, and practiced, over and over again until it is done quickly and perfectly.

This is why, during the six months they train under Broderick's direction, the Marines of the 24th MEU seem to be constantly breathing hard.

For the safe evacuation of civilians, as for each of these operations, the playbook suggests how the operation should be organized: in what order the sniper teams, medical teams, and food supplies should hit the landing zone, how and when the teams should communicate with each other and with the ground commander, and how the evacuees and the Marines can be flown out without leaving anyone behind.

The playbook, in essence, is a record of past failures and successes and a method of making successes work faster. From the 1983 bombing of the 24th MEU's barracks in Beirut, for instance, has come tightened security techniques and simplified lines of command. From past experience with garbled orders and reports has come a standardized one-word code system for monitoring the process of the operation.

"Seahawks" means the force has been inserted successfully. "Yankees" means the force has been extracted and everyone is accounted for.

In Desert Storm, U.S. forces had months to plan in excruciating detail. In Somalia, the 24th MEU will be asked to do complicated operations in less than thirty minutes.

"Everything we do is built around crisis response," says Truman "Butch" Preston, a lieutenant colonel who serves as Broderick's second-in-command.

"You look at things you might have to do, you think them through and what-if them to death," he explains. "You have go no-go criteria. You try to eliminate the possibilities of what can go wrong. You try to keep it simple. And you establish SOPs [standard operating procedures] so that while the planners are working out the details, you can get your people doing rehearsals, drawing ammunition, getting ready."

After an operation is launched, Murphy usually shows up, Preston says. "It's night, your adrenaline and pucker factor are pretty high, and when your communications go down and things go wrong, there's a tendency to wing it. But if you have thought it through, everybody knows what they're doing, your decision-making is decentralized, and it works."

The playbook and operational strategy change over time. Broderick is already getting reports back from the Marines sent earlier to Somalia about what works and what doesn't, and what to emphasize in his training (more crowd control and police work, for instance). Broderick's own experience with these operations goes back to the evacuation of the U.S. embassy in Saigon in 1975, when he was a young captain.

"What doesn't change," says Broderick, "is the way we operate. Tactics are based on saving lives.

"Look, in this job, probably more than in any other job, we eat, sleep, live with these kids," he says, speaking about his Marines. "On a four-hole shitter out there, I'm banging knees with Corporal Smith. There's no difference between us. We live in confined quarters. I love these kids, literally. So the last thing I want to see is their faces in body bags.

"I spend a lot of time worrying about it," says Broderick, who at forty-six is the father of three daughters and grandfather to four children.

When Broderick convenes his staff at 0900, it's a short meeting. Gathered around him are the officers who handle communications, logistics, maintenance, intelligence, operations; his infantry battalion commander and his staff; and his air squadron officers. Except for the aviators, all wear camouflage utilities, and many have wads of tobacco tucked behind their lower lips (and carry Styrofoam coffee cups to spit in). The aviators wear one-piece olive-drab flight suits and jaunty leather flight jackets. They shun tobacco.

George Fenton runs the meeting, it seems, through clenched teeth. A lieutenant colonel, he is Broderick's operations officer.

Fenton is brusque, abrupt. He is responsible for keeping this briefing short and businesslike. Fenton's maternal grandfather was a Marine general, his paternal grandfather a career Marine officer. His father, Francis "Ike" Fenton, fought in World War II and Korea and Vietnam. George's uncle, a Marine private, was killed in battle with the Japanese on Okinawa.

Fenton lays out the scenario. He invites suggestions on how the problem might be handled. It is a tense but collegial atmosphere. Every Marine officer is a trained ground combat leader, whether his subsequent

George Fenton, with a Korean War photo of his father,
Marine Capt. Francis "Ike" Fenton.

speciality is aviation or logistics or computer networking. Everyone's
ideas and opinions are heard.

Landing the Marines by boat is ruled out because of high seas. The
aviation guys say they can support a helo operation.

Much time is spent defining the "rules of engagement," which spec-
ify how much force can be used in what kinds of situations. Should the
Marines go in with weapons loaded? Shoot rioters on sight or only to defend their own lives? Are warning shots into the air authorized? Or is only
nonlethal force authorized?

The Marines, after all, are exhaustively trained in using nonlethal
force in confronting mobs. They are hardened to ignore taunts and rocks
without flinching. They can charge at double- or triple-time in a diamond-
shaped phalanx into an unruly crowd, shouting in unison each time their
left feet touch the ground. They can arrange their formation to enclose a
"snatch team" which can dart out, tackle a mob leader, wrestle him to the

ground, and handcuff him while the formation closes protectively around the team. In extreme mob situations the Marines fix bayonets and charge. The bayonets are of little use in actual combat, but they "scare the bejesus out of people," says Gunnery Sergeant Andrew Dillard, an expert in riot control.

Broderick leans back in his chair, listening intently. A Rite-Aid Interdental Stimulator, an oversize toothpick, wriggles and squirms between his lips. (Broderick's radio call sign is "Chomper" for his onetime habit of chewing on cigars. He has reluctantly given them up. Instead, he will chew to splinters many boxes of Rite-Aids in the months ahead.)

Broderick at last sits up. He sets the rules of engagement: Marines go with weapons unloaded; they can use lethal force only in extreme situations to save their own lives. He assigns Mark Toal, the captain of Charlie Company, to carry out the mission. Broderick wants Toal's detailed plan back here in forty-five minutes.

"This is a plain and simple NEO," says Broderick, using the acronym for noncombatant evacuation operation. "I don't wanna get bogged down in there, I don't wanna get decisively engaged. In and out before dark."

Any questions? It is 0916. Launch is set for 1300, one o'clock. When Broderick says, "Okay, let's go, guys," chairs scrape back, people fly out the door.

Mark Toal is a tall, angular thirty-year-old from Milwaukee. He has high cheekbones, and when he finds something funny or incredible, which is often, his blue eyes pop open wide and his toothy grin stretches past his cheekbones and back toward his ears. Toal is a captain, a hard-earned rank he has reached after long years as a lowly lieutenant, as an instructor at infantry officers' school where he taught new lieutenants, as a Marine Corps recruiter, and as a student himself at the Amphibious Warfare School, the first level of graduate school for Marine officers.

Charlie Company is his first big combat command. He is determined not to blow it. Not because he is ambitious ("I am not a career Marine," he insists). But because he has watched other company commanders make mistakes.

A few weeks ago on a live-fire exercise, a young lieutenant allowed a squad to get too far forward. Two men were mistakenly shot and wounded. Broderick held a brief inquiry, then summarily removed the lieutenant and a sergeant from command, a humiliating disgrace that effectively ended their careers. "We don't fuck around with Marines' lives," Broderick explained. "They didn't think clearly. The lieutenant wasn't paying attention to detail. He was irresponsible. It was a young kid's mistake. But we don't have a lot of empathy for him."

It is not just fear that stimulates Mark Toal. It is that he loves his Marines and wants to do well for them. Because it is the right thing to do.

A newspaper reporter once called Toal "earnest" in print. Now his men fondly call him "Captain Earnest." Behind his back, they say he is the best company commander they've ever had.

Right now Toal is sweating hard. He has forty-five minutes to come up with a detailed plan that will pass Broderick's demanding standards. With a handful of colored markers, he attacks a stack of overhead projector transparencies, or TPs, that he will use to brief the MEU on his plan.

Toal starts by assigning his squads and platoons to various tasks. Then, working backward, he figures out the order in which they must land and then groups them into units, or "sticks," of helo passengers. He has a half-dozen helos to work with; if one malfunctions, he must decide which sticks can be dropped from the mission. Which sticks must carry which equipment. MREs. Water. Extra helmets and flak jackets for the evacuees. How much ammo? Radios. Passwords and call signs: Toal is "Badger." The overall mission commander, who will remain back at headquarters monitoring the operation, is "Nightstalker." If a helo goes down in hostile territory, Toal must have a team (and a helo) standing by to rescue the men and fix the helo.

He summons his right-hand man, First Sergeant Willie Wilkerson. Have the platoon sergeants run through the scenarios. Check the radio gear. Brief the men on the rules of engagement, including no talking to the press.

As the minutes sweep toward 1100, Toal grabs his TPs and maps and notes and hustles next door where Broderick and the other MEU officers are settling in for a final meeting before the operation commences. This is called a confirmation brief. Each member of the staff must confirm that he can do his part: the air squadron that it can deliver the required number of helos; the commo guys that the communications links will work; the logistics guys that they have provided and packed medical kits, stretchers, MREs, water, and the dozens of other items required.

Fenton whips the meeting along.

"Okay, S-2 [intelligence], anything new?"

"No sir, situation remains the same."

"Check. Comm?"

Marine briefer.

"Sir, Comm can support. Here's my comm plan." The comm officer projects his TP on the wall. Broderick studies it. The diagram shows three alternate means of communicating, plus one option if all communications fail: various colored flares. Broderick's Rite-Aid is jumping. "Okay," he says.

Toal briefs his plan. A hundred pairs of eyes examine his TPs, looking for problems and errors. At 1400, says Toal, seven CH-46 helos will begin hitting Landing Zone Raven, each carrying a stick of nine Marines. Two squads will deploy here, four there. The plan includes two alternate escape-and-evasion routes, in case disaster strikes and Toal's Marines have to make their own way out.

At one point Broderick interrupts. "Okay, now that we've confused the whole fucking room, let's go through this all again so everybody knows what the hell we're doing."

When Toal finishes, Fenton leaps up and calls on each officer to yea or nay the plan. Toal stands and sweats, twisting his pointer in his hands. When everyone has had his say, Fenton says, "Colonel?" and sits down.

Broderick sits up, removes some splinters from his mouth, and inserts a fresh Rite-Aid.

Charlie Company landing, exercise, Camp Lejeune.

"What are ya gonna do if the bad guys show up there at your LZ?" he demands, pointing at Toal's sketch of the landing zone.

"Sir, we'll divert to our alternate LZ over here." Toal indicates with his pointer. He waits and sweats. Finally Broderick nods slowly.

"There's a lot of Murphys in your alternate plan; let's hope we don't have to use it," he says.

"Roger that, sir," says Toal.

A few hours later, Charlie Company hits the LZ like an army of space invaders gone amok. They are forty minutes late because the helo pilots had misunderstood and were waiting for the Marines at the wrong pickup point. ("You gotta let whatever they tell you blow in one ear and out the other," says a tall lance corporal named Eddie Adams, lying on the ground at the pickup point, with his head resting on his helmet, waiting for the helo to show up. "Never believe anything until it actually happens.")

Now Charlie Company thunders down out of the sky in huge, steel-gray CH-46 helicopters whose twin blades madly beat the air. With a deafening roar, the machines flare into a soccer field, lower their ramps, and disgorge streams of Marines who sprint across the grass, fling themselves on the ground beneath a low wall, and peer out over their weapons. They wear helmets and black gloves; brown and green camouflage paint is smeared across their faces. In seconds, the helos power up and slide away, the fierce downdraft peppering the prone Marines with supersonic pebbles and twigs.

Toal is up and running. His men fan out to form a security perimeter; others dart down a street like leaves blowing in an autumn wind, eddying up against a church wall, at the corner of a house and in the shadow of what looks like a city hall building.

This is Combat Town, a mock village built on the edge of Camp Lejeune for war games. Toal kneels, lifts the microphone of the heavy radio he is carrying on his back, and speaks softly: "Nightstalker, Badger. Seahawks."

Almost immediately, there is trouble.

Gangs of men (played by off-duty Marines) gather in knots, taunting the Marines. A few rocks sail through the air. These exercise rocks are real. The Marines gulp and duck but hold steady.

The "mayor" of the town appears, shouting angrily in a fake Middle Eastern accent (he, too, is an off-duty Marine). "Who are you people?

Mark Toal, Combat Town.

What right do you have?" he demands, playing his role with gusto. The mayor has his own security force, men in black raincoats carrying weapons. They gesture menacingly at the Marines. The American ambassador, who is supposed to have gathered Americans for evacuation, cannot be found. Toal cannot raise the U.S. embassy on his radio.

"Somebody's going to get shot!" the mayor yells.

Toal's men gradually impose order. Toal speaks quietly with the mayor and reaches an accommodation. Marines start bringing in groups of American civilians to be evacuated. They are logged in, searched for weapons, and given a cursory medical check. One "evacuee" is PFC Michael ("911") Rosenberger. He is playing a whiny American teenager.

"I wanna cigarette," he whines. "Gimme a cigarette."

"Let's just get your name and address down here, pal," says a Marine patiently.

"Gimme a cigarette first," Rosenberger demands.

The Marine sighs heavily and fishes in his pocket.

"Captain, this man needs immediate evacuation." Charlie Company's corpsman confronts Toal. An American civilian has been shot. He is writhing in simulated pain. The corpsman has bound his "wound" and put him on a stretcher.

Marines occupy church, Combat Town.

"Roger that," says Toal, and speaks into his radio. In twelve minutes, the man is on his way on a helo.

Toal gets another report: There are wounded Americans a mile away just inside a tree line. It could be an ambush; the rebel forces are not far away. Toal details a platoon to go have a look.

"Be careful!" he calls as they trot out into the dusk. Then he sighs. "So many things can go wrong," he says.

In fact, things go relatively well. The Marines stoically face down the mobs. Toal's platoon is not ambushed. The ambassador is found. Helos

Off-duty Marines play local goons in exercise, Combat Town.

Jonathan Blackwell, sentry duty, Combat Town.

cycle in and carry off groups of evacuees. The Marines shrink their perimeter. First Sergeant Wilkerson carefully checks off each Marine as he boards a helo. Just before he leaves, the last man out, Toal picks up his radio to advise Broderick that Charlie Company is out safe.

"Nightstalker, Badger."

Static.

"Nightstalker, Badger."

Static.

Toal curses. *"Nightstalker, Badger!"*

"Nightstalker," says the static.

"Nightstalker, Badger. Yankees," says Toal.

The operation has unfolded under the narrow eyes of a Marine Corps trainer. He has taken many notes. Now, in a late-night meeting, he leads the MEU officers in a critique of their performance.

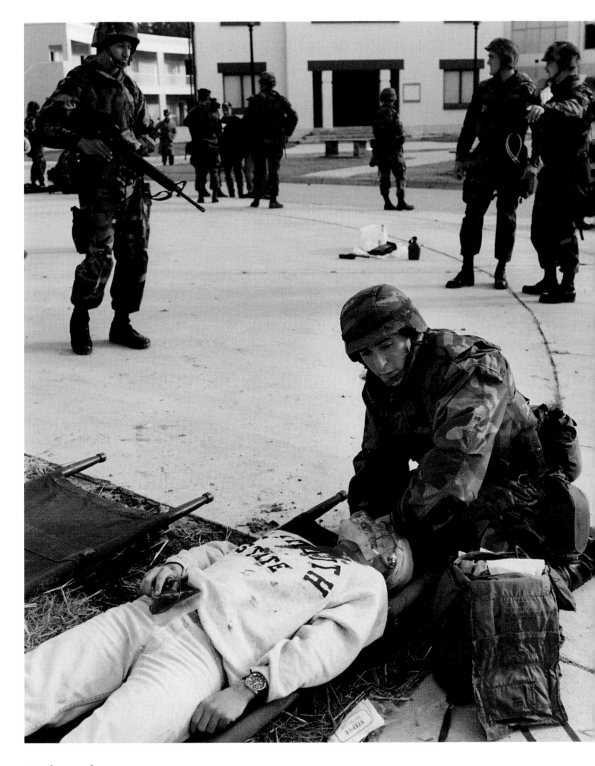

Mock casualty.

John Wesling.

Toal: "We went in too aggressive. We should have gone in with no face paint and with our weapons slung. One thing I learned, you have to coordinate with the local mayor. It would help if we had the rules of engagement printed up on cards for the troops."

"At ease, guys," Broderick growls at some chatter at the back of the room. "This is our last chance to get it right."

The air commander apologizes for his pilots waiting at the wrong

Charlie Company shrinks its perimeter.

pickup point. "I should have alerted the colonel when we were late," he says.

Broderick: "That's important because [in a real operation] I'm on the phone with the White House and Colin Powell wants to know what's happening."

"You're right about the way you went in," the trainer, Lieutenant Colonel Rick Tryon, tells Toal. "If you come off the helos like gangbusters, that alone could panic a benign environment. Your leaders should do an assessment on the ground before you send your men fanning out. And you need to designate somebody to deal with CNN."

Roger that, murmurs Broderick. For he knows that out on a "real-

Ray Grundy.

world" operation, he will be under as much pressure and scrutiny from the media as the politicians back in Washington.

If his men screw up, Washington and the world will know about it perhaps sooner than Broderick himself.

Operating under the media's watchful eyes isn't the only thing worrying Broderick. It's the not-quite-war, definitely-not-peace aspect of the Somalia operation itself.

"We don't just jump into a place and shoot people, like in the movies," he says. "But see, this is the dilemma of Somalia. I'm used to seizing the goddamn runway from the bad guys. Now, what if the bad guys there are just sitting on their guns?

"You plan for the worst case, and you go in fast, you use speed, shock, stealth, to limit the potential for a firefight, to get in and out before the bad guys have time to get organized.

"It puts an awful lot of responsibility on these kids. They're the ones out there doing it. And they're pretty damn good," Broderick says with feeling.

The exercises go on day and night. When they are over, in mid-February, Broderick kicks his men out for twelve days of leave. Many stay right here at Camp Lejeune with their families. Hundreds of others ride taxis out past the Dollhouse to the airport, bound for reunions with their parents and girlfriends. (In a lonely garage at the edge of Lejeune, however, the crew of the Hell Bitch works straight through leave, trying to work out mechanical problems before they ship out. "I didn't have time to talk to my wife and kids or nothing," says Jon Flores. "It was twenty-hour days, then—bam!—gone.")

The rest of them, after twelve giddy days of wives and children, late nights and beer parties and sleeping late, reluctantly pull on their boots and utilities, shoulder their seabags, and assemble at the edge of the hard, glittering sea a few miles up the coast from Camp Lejeune.

It is not a dramatic departure: Families are not allowed at the bustling pier from which they leave. There are no flags or bands or television cameras.

They huddle against an icy wind as they stand waiting for their turn to board the landing craft that will ferry them out to their ships. There is little of the boisterous grab-ass that usually erupts among idle Marines. Yet there is a sense of excitement and adventure in the air. After all the training, the real world awaits.

Kenny Joe Hebert, a lanky twenty-one-year-old from New Iberia, La., stuffs a wad of Red Man tobacco into his mouth and ponders the future. He is looking forward to it.

"What with all the practicing we do," he drawls, "not going on a real-world operation is kinda like sleeping with a woman without having sex. When we get to Somalia or wherever, guys are going to be fighting to be the first ones out."

But older hands know different.

"That's naive ignorance. They don't know enough to be scared," says Ray Grundy, standing disconsolately nearby. Gunner Grundy is the MEU's forty-three-year-old weapons officer; hence the respected title of "Gunner" (as distinct from "Gunny," or gunnery sergeant). He is a chief warrant officer, an enlisted Marine who has risen through the ranks and gained a technical expertise that is recognized with officer rank. (Unlike other officers, however, warrant officers cannot lead troops.)

Gunner Grundy has been a Marine for twenty-four years. He has fought in Vietnam and other trouble spots. He has said good-bye many times. Now that he is married and his son Matthew is four years old, it is getting harder. Grundy has been gone for half the boy's life.

Only one leave-taking, Grundy is thinking, was more painful than this one. It was in the fall of 1990 and Grundy was en route to Saudi Arabia to help drive the Iraqis out of Kuwait. Marines were staging to go, standing around in the bitter cold at Camp Lejeune, just like now. An officer came by, handing out injectors containing antidotes in case the Marines were hit with deadly nerve gas.

"I talked to my boy. I told him to be a good boy for Mommy. My wife was bawling. Holding me. I said good-bye and they left. It was the hardest thing I have ever done. I will always carry with me the picture of those red taillights going down the street, and me thinking that I'll probably never see these people again.

"And then, like any good Marine, I turned and shook it off and got on about the business we're paid to do."

The 24th MEU sails from Camp Lejeune on February 24, 1993, 2,100 Marines and all their gear, including the Hell Bitch and its exhausted crew. In Somalia the following day, three Marines are wounded in a series of battles in which Somali gunmen attack UN offices, the U.S. diplomatic mission, international aid facilities, and hotels housing foreigners. The story runs on page A-27 of the *Washington Post*. Most of the newspaper is filled with news of President Clinton's budget plan and arguments over taxes and spending.

As the Marines sail, Washington's attention is turned elsewhere.

QUESTION: Do you think the Marine Corps has gotten too soft (by making boot camp less harsh, by going to four-man dorm rooms instead of barracks, by allowing women and beer in the rooms, etc.)?

Only the part about boot camp. The rest (beer and women) is needed. We're humans, ya know.
—Lance Corporal, Infantry

No. The Marine Corps still holds many of its values from the old Corps, i.e., military discipline and personal bearing, esprit de corps and a motivation level higher than other branches [of service]. The willingness and ability to endure dangerous and harsh situations seems always to be the hallmark of a Marine. I believe the pride and discipline of a Marine is unmatched and always will be. Semper Fi!
—Lance Corporal, Artillery

Yes. Boot camp is way too easy. Beer and women in the barracks is good— work hard and play hard. Plus, before they made that rule [to allow beer and women in the barracks] we had them in there anyway.
—Lance Corporal, Mortars

If you have seen how ridiculous the rules are for women in the room, you wouldn't really ask that. The blinds must be open, [women can] only visit between certain hours and are not allowed in the head. Yes, you don't want girl- friends living in the barracks sponging off the gov't, but we need time alone for some privacy, maybe rack ops, you know what I mean. Hotels get expensive.
—Corporal, Aviation Technician

5

DEATH STAR
USS WASP, ATLANTIC OCEAN
February 1993

At sea, Eddie Adams's rack is his home.

It is roughly thirty-six inches wide and eighty-four inches long, and it is bolted at the top of a tier of three racks. On tiptoe, Adams can just manage to reach up and tug his sheet and blanket taut and precisely square his pillow according to Marine Corps standards (exactly six inches of topsheet turned down over the blanket). Adams is six foot three. His rack is the top one in a tier of three. When he swings his frame up into his rack, he can draw a set of orange curtains and snap on his overhead reading light. But he can't sit up: three feet above his mattress is a maze of high-pressure pipes and wiring and air ducts, all painted the same dust-yellow. When he climbs up to his rack after a long day, Adams customarily wads his pillow up under his head, lies on his side and spends a few delicious minutes with his favorite book, the Bible.

Adams's rack, a space little larger than a coffin, is his own personal, precious space, an inviolable cocoon. When he is in the rack, he can escape for a while being Lance Corporal Eddie Adams, a rifleman in Charlie Company, 1st Battalion, 2nd Marines. He can forget that he is boxed up in enlisted berthing, deep inside a maze of steel passageways and decks and bulkheads and compartments packed with lethal weapons and ammunition and fuel and helicopters and three thousand other people, all plowing along through the Atlantic Ocean aboard the USS *Wasp* toward Somalia.

In his rack, he is just Eddie Adams, twenty-two years old, a fresh-faced boy from the town of Leeds in central Alabama, a kid with a troubled past and a bright future.

Reveille sounds at 0600. A boatswain's whistle pierces the night. "Reveille reveille reveille, all hands heave out," a sailor announces on the ship's loudspeaker system, called the "1MC."

Adams lies inert on his back for a minute or two. Then he props himself up on his elbows, swings his legs over the side, and leaps, landing with a thud on the vibrating linoleum-covered steel deck that forms a three-foot aisle between Adams's rack and the next tier. The aisle is cluttered with boots and boxes and crowded with people.

Adams fumbles for his shower togs, collects the towel hanging from a pipe above his rack, and heads off to the showers. There are five stainless steel shower stalls and forty grumpy Marines, grousing and scratching and farting, cramming into the head to use the urinals, waiting for a shower, elbowing in at the sinks for a shave. A decade ago, *Wasp*'s designers, at the Ingalls shipyard in Pascagoula, Miss., labored mightily to get vast amounts of fresh air pumped in here. They have only partially succeeded. The air hangs heavy with the peculiar aroma of warships: sweaty clothes, grease, diesel exhaust, floor wax, wet paper towels, steam-table food, Brasso metal polish, unwashed socks, and gun oil.

"Death Star."

From his rack, Adams can be anywhere on the ship in three or four minutes. If there is an operation about to get underway, he will leap out of his rack at 0400 and fumble for his gear in the red glow of *Wasp*'s night lighting. He will bound down the steep steel stairway to the deck below, joining a stream of helmeted Marines with packs and rifles bumping and jostling along a narrow passageway, slowing to squeeze through a hatchway and eddying around a dungareed sailor unlucky enough to be coming the wrong way.

The stream of men will empty into enlisted mess, a basketball court–size dining hall that is hot and noisy almost twenty-four hours a day (250 people sit here at a time, gulping their food in four or five minutes and escaping elsewhere). The stream will wind past tables and benches and past sailors balancing trays of food, flow into another narrow passageway that runs past the bustling kitchens and sculleries, and empty out into the vast cavern of the hangar deck.

Resupply.

Enlisted mess. Kenny Joe Hebert, center.

Hangar deck.

The hangar deck echoes like a giant warehouse. Two sixteen-ton CH-53 helos sit at one end aswarm with mechanics; at the other, a Harrier attack jet is coming in for an overhaul. A small tractor tugs and backs the forty-six-foot-long Harrier into position. Forklift trucks growl back and forth carrying pallets of spare parts. On either side, three-story-high doors have been slid back fifty feet so that aircraft can be rolled out to an elevator which will lift them up to the flight deck. More important, the open doors give Adams and the other Marines a rare glimpse and sniff of the outside world.

If an operation is underway, Adams and the other Marines will wait here, "staged" to ride either helos or Hovercraft, called LCAC ("el-cacks"), to shore. If it is helos, the men will be organized into sticks; their platoon leaders will check off their names, ID numbers, and blood types on a clipboard, and they will head up a steep internal ramp and wait again before getting the "Go Go Go!" and sprinting out into the fresh air and commotion of the flight deck.

If it is LCACs, they will head from the hangar deck down a steep internal ramp, turn a corner, and trudge down another ramp onto the Hovercraft, squeezed in a line of three into *Wasp's* football field–size well deck, their turbine engines screeching and firing out plumes of black exhaust. Once the Marines are on board, *Wasp* will suck fifteen thousand tons of seawater into its aft tanks, settle in the water, open its stern gate, and release the LCACs like a goose laying eggs.

Underway, the LCACs resemble giant, mutant water bugs. Cloaked in clouds of spray and exhaust fumes, the LCACs buzz along on top of the water on black rubber air cushions that pulsate and glisten, while their long antennae wave and their windshield wipers flick like cilia.

But this is a more normal day at sea. By 0645 Adams has finished chow (oatmeal, pancakes, bacon, an apple, two glasses of milk). At 0700 he stands formation with his platoon. They sit through a class on land mines, then spend two hours field-daying their quarters. *Field-day* is a Marine verb that originally referred to a day of cleaning, polishing, and scrubbing. It now simply means "to clean." Lunch at 1100 (turkey à la king). Then the hours begin to stretch. At 1600, *Wasp's* 179 closed-circuit TV sets blink to life with eight hours of movies and taped TV shows: *Maverick*, *Leave It to Beaver*, *Donahue*, and *The Terminator*, starring Arnold Schwarzenegger.

At 2200, or 10 P.M., the 1MC carries the evening prayer and a brief

LCAC (Landing Craft, Air Cushion) backs away from *Wasp*'s stern.

Enlisted berthing.

announcement: "Lights out!" Most of the *Wasp*'s internal lights flicker to red. Activity goes on without pause. Down the aisle from where Adams is reading the Bible, two Marines are thumbing through a dog-eared *Penthouse* magazine. Somebody has the ironing board out and is trying to flatten the wrinkles in his camouflage utilities.

Further along, where the aisle opens up into a common area with tables and chairs and a TV set, Kenny Joe Hebert is playing hearts and spitting tobacco juice into an empty soda can. Jose Rocha, sweating heavily from pumping iron in the weight room, is watching Wrestlemania III. Steve Conway, twenty-two, is wolfing down Pringles potato chips and trying to get Carl Chapman, who is polishing his boots, to listen to a story about his ex-wife.

The Marines are tenants—squatters, really—on this huge ship. The *Wasp* is owned by the United States Navy and it is run by sailors. Sailors are different from Marines (in their separate slang, they are "squids" and "jarheads"). For one thing, squids don't go through the crucible of Marine Corps boot camp. Nor do they live in tight communities like Camp Lejeune. Jarheads believe that squids are a little less disciplined than Marines, a little less physically fit, a little more slovenly. Squids wear dungarees and denim shirts and work boots; Marines sport combat utilities and polished

Danny Fish, *Wasp* metal shop.

black boots. It is a little like cramming Republicans and Democrats together in the same crowded election-night ballroom.

Still, they manage to work together. Squids work in Danny Fish's metal shop just aft of the hanger deck. Fish is a Marine sergeant. He is twenty-nine and has a friendly gap-toothed smile. Up on the flight deck recently, the wind whipped a helo rotor into the side of the bird, creating a long gash. The helo was hauled below, where Fish and his men replaced the smashed piece of fuselage, working twenty-nine hours straight to fashion the plate and struts, weld it in, and polish it down to an undetectable finish. Then they made a new fuel tank for a Jeep and fashioned a four-foot-high candleholder for the ship chapel.

"Our guys are shit-hot," Fish says proudly.

Squids also work with Marine Corporal Robert Wilson in the avionics shop, maintaining and repairing the electronic components in aircraft.

Wilson is in a bad mood. "Half the stuff I work on is older than I am," he gripes. Wilson is twenty-six. "You come out on a float like this doing your job, the women think you're abandoning them. Aah," says this old-timer, "things just ain't what they used to be."

The one place that Adams and other enlisted men can't wander around, unless they're on official business, is upstairs in officers' country. Officers' quarters are called "staterooms," though there is nothing stately about them. Captain Mark Toal, for instance, lives in a four-man stateroom that measures ten feet by ten feet; most of that space is taken up by racks (two-tiered bunks). There is a tiny washbasin, two fold-down desks, and storage area for helmets, flak jackets, and field packs. Damp towels hang from the ceiling below the air-conditioning vent.

The officers' other amenity is the wardroom. The food here is sometimes a cut above enlisted mess, but the real benefits are that the food is served, and the atmosphere is quiet. Squid and jarhead officers help themselves at the salad bar and find a seat at one of the long, white-clothed tables where mess boys—both squids and temporarily assigned Marines—bring them a main course and dessert.

It is up on the flight deck, though, that squids and jarheads really work together in the dangerous, complicated ballet that attends the launching and recovery of aircraft. By today's supercarrier standards, *Wasp* is a shrimp. Its flight deck is 819 feet long, two-thirds the length of a supercarrier like the *America* and about the size of a World War II carrier. (*Wasp*'s namesake, the eighth in a line of famed Navy *Wasp*s, was sunk during the 1942 battle of Guadalcanal.)

This *Wasp* was built smallish on purpose. It is an amphibious assault carrier. Most of the Navy's aircraft carriers were built to conduct operations in midocean; they have long flight decks to accommodate heavy supersonic jets that were built to fly long distances and dogfight with sophisticated jets defending the Soviet Union. *Wasp* was built to haul Marines close in to the beach, to launch them and their gear in boats and helicopters, and to support them with helicopters and Harrier attack jets.

The *Wasp* can sit offshore, or wait just over the horizon, for months. Then, when needed, she can land her Marine combat power ashore with stunning speed and sustain it in combat for weeks. She can get the Marines and all their vehicles and gear back on board in less than a day and a half, then steam away to another trouble spot.

The Marines, in awe of the *Wasp*'s combat power, call her the "Death

Chicago Public Library

Independence

2/26/2011   2:30:16 PM

-Patron Receipt-

ITEMS BORROWED:

1:
Title: My FBI : bringing down the Mafia, in
Item #: R0405290696
Due Date: 3/19/2011

2:
Title: Alligators in the sewer and 222 other
Item #: R0303705173
Due Date: 3/19/2011

3:
Title: Captain Trips : a biography of Jerry G
Item #: R0110242281
Due Date: 3/19/2011

-Please retain for your records-

Star." The first thing Marines tell a newcomer to enlisted berthing is that Nostradamus, the sixteenth-century French astrologer, predicted four hundred years ago that a ship named after an insect, the tenth ship of that name and the first of its class, would sink in the Persian Gulf in 1993 (the *Wasp* fits all those categories save the last). The enlisted Marines are also convinced the *Wasp* has a fatal crack along her keel. Every night, they say, the crack has to be secretly rewelded. The ship's officers have given up trying to deny the crack-in-the-hull rumor.

The *Wasp* cost American taxpayers a billion dollars and appears to be worth every cent. But when she was launched in 1987, it was to the sound of smirks and raspberries from the naval peanut gallery. Let the *Wasp*, with its slow and fat Harrier "jump-jets," piddle around in shallow water. The real Navy would master the high seas and the world.

The smirking has stopped. The Cold War is over and the Navy has officially declared that its purpose now is to master not the high seas or the Soviet Union, but the close-in coastal areas the *Wasp* was built for. The captains of the unwieldy supercarriers are eyeing *Wasp* with new respect. (And the Navy, to nobody's apparent satisfaction, is experimenting with putting Marine detachments on the supercarriers.)

"The ship is at flight quarters!" barks the 1MC as the boatswain's whistle fades. "All hands not involved in flight operations stand clear of the flight deck, weather decks, and catwalks!"

Mad Dog Moore clamps on his helmet and clumps up the steel stairs to the flight deck. Mad Dog is flying today. He grew up in Cadiz, Ky. He is the kind of farm boy who can instinctively build, fix, drive, or fly anything. He once restored a '53 Harley. It was featured in a national motorcycle magazine. After college, Marine Corps infantry officers' school, flight school, and several years of operational experience, he is Lieutenant Robert H. Moore, USMC. He is a CH-46 helicopter pilot.

Mad Dog, wearing his olive-drab, flame-resistant flight suit, gloves, and floatation vest, stomps around his bird, doing his preflight check. He glares suspiciously at hydraulic connections for leaks, checks oil levels, and tugs on wires to make sure nothing is loose.

The '46 is an ungainly mass of mottled gray metal. It looks something like a frog; in fact, Marines call it a Frog. This Frog is the *Ragin' Cajun*. Its crew chief, Kenneth Troy Dane McGuffee, has given it that name and caused it to be painted on the Frog's fuselage. As crew chief, McGuffee is responsible for this helo's maintenance; he certifies that it is

Mad Dog.

Kenneth Troy Dane ("Gruff Dawg") McGuffee.

safe to fly, and in flight, he supervises everything on it from the pilots' seats on back. He is twenty-four and has fled the short horizons of his hometown of Pistol Thicket, La.

The *Ragin' Cajun* has twin rotors fore and aft, a rear loading ramp, four round windows along the fuselage, and a small door on either side just aft of the pilots' seats where machine guns can be mounted. Along the fuselage are memories of Vietnam: bullet holes that have been hurriedly patched and repatched. There are scars of other battles, too: gouges and stains and nicks and dents. This helicopter was built in 1967, when Mad Dog was a toddler of twenty-four months.

Now he hoists himself up into the helo and squeezes into the left front seat, fastening his lap and shoulder harness. While he sets his radio frequencies and checks his fire handles (pushed in), circuit breakers (off), battery switch (on), and a hundred other details, a deck crewman attaches a tow bar and tractor to the helo and pulls Mad Dog out from his parking slot to the edge of the flight deck. Mad Dog sets his brakes and reaches up and hits the auxiliary-power-unit switch overhead.

The APU, or "ape," sounds like a giant vacuum cleaner. It slowly winds up to a shrieking whoosh that Eddie Adams can hear down in his rack. With the APU running hot, Mad Dog and his copilot start each of the helo's two turboshaft engines, watching engine temperature and oil pressure come up to their proper settings. Next, they check to make sure the deck crew is standing clear, and Mad Dog drops the rotor blade brake lever at his right thigh and pushes his two throttles forward to full RPMs.

This is a check-out ride; no troops are to be loaded. Mad Dog raises *Ragin' Cajun*'s rear ramp. The helo is shaking and roaring, its blades thwacking into the wind, straining to lift off. Mad Dog's attention is now riveted on the helmeted figure standing thirty feet in front of his windshield. This is the flight director. He wears a yellow shirt to be immediately distinguishable from the mechanics (blue shirts), ordnance men (red shirts), and fuel handlers (purple shirts).

Yellow Shirt, a very experienced senior squid, communicates with Mad Dog by hand signals. He holds a clenched fist high in the air (this signals Mad Dog to stay put), and with the other, points to two deckhands standing back behind the flight deck's safety line, well away from *Ragin' Cajun*'s whirling blades. The two men sprint beneath the helo and unhook four heavy chains holding it to the deck. They sprint bent over around to the front of the helo and hold the chains up for Mad Dog to see. He counts four chains and nods. (If Mad Dog tried to take off with one chain still holding one of his wheels to the deck, the helo would flip on its side, smashing its blades into the deck, throwing off pieces of debris, and exploding in a fireball. It is only one of the many things that can go wrong.)

Now Yellow Shirt holds his arms outstretched horizontally and flicks his fingers up. In the cockpit, Mad Dog throttles up. Behind him, McGuffee has his head out the doorway making sure everything is clear, and occasionally ducking inside to scan the hoses and pipes that crisscross the interior for leaks. McGuffee gives Mad Dog the all-clear. Mad Dog thumbs-up to Yellow Shirt. Yellow Shirt double-checks to make sure all his deck hands are back behind the safety line. Then he holds his arms outstretched and vigorously lifts them several times over his head.

Mad Dog has his hands positioned on two controls. On his left is the collective. It changes the angle at which each blade bites into the air. At idle on the flight deck, the blades' pitch is nearly flat. Now he pulls the collective up, and the whirling blades chew into the air. Mad Dog's other hand is on the cyclic, between his knees. It changes the blades' pitch on one side of the aircraft or the other, causing the helo to bank left or right. Mad Dog nudges the cyclic to the left. This will bank the *Ragin' Cajun* slightly to the left, into the wind, keeping it steady.

As Mad Dog nudges his collective, the helo lurches unevenly off the deck. At ten feet, Mad Dog scans his instruments, watching for an over-heating engine. This is critical: If the helo is overloaded, if it is taking too much power to get off the deck, this is the point it has to be put down and troops unloaded. But this time, Mad Dog is satisfied. So is Yellow Shirt, who has been checking the belly of the helo for leaks or any other prob-lems. McGuffee, on the intercom, calls, "Clear to slide left." Mad Dog massages his controls, and the helo rises and slides left, leaving the edge of the flight deck.

Now, Mad Dog is flying. He puts the nose down and leaves the *Wasp* behind, climbing at two hundred feet per minute. At two hundred feet he calls the tower, giving his flight call sign.

"Thunder one two, operations normal, left out."

The tower curtly acknowledges.

"One plus three zero," says Mad Dog, reporting that he has one hour and thirty minutes of fuel on board, "and four souls," indicating there are four people on board.

"Roger that," says the tower.

When Mad Dog recovers to the *Wasp*, he will fly up alongside the ship and hover just seaward of his assigned LZ. Yellow Shirt will be there on the flight deck. He will signal Mad Dog to slide right, positioning him precisely before allowing him to settle on the deck. McGuffee and the other crewman will be watching out their windows, talking Mad Dog down into position on the deck.

With a clenched fist in the air, Yellow Shirt will hold Mad Dog there, blades whirling, while two deckhands spring forward and chain the *Ragin' Cajun* to the deck. They will spring around in front of Mad Dog and hold up their empty arms, so that Mad Dog knows he is chained down. Finally, Yellow Shirt will signal Mad Dog to shut down his engines. As the blades coast to a stop, men will rush forward to tie down the drooping blades so they won't smack into somebody or something in the wind.

It would be complicated and dangerous enough if Mad Dog had the

Parked helos, *Wasp* flight deck.

flight deck to himself. But there are eleven other '46s here, parked along the starboard edge of the flight deck, their tails extended far out over the water. Three giant CH-53 helicopters are also parked here (the fourth is down in the hangar deck), along with three Huey helos and four Cobra helicopter gunships.

At the aft end of the flight deck, five Harrier attack jets are also parked, waiting for the *Ragin' Cajun* to be trundled back to its parking place so that the flight deck is clear for jet operations. Pacing back and forth along the flight deck are Dave Tierney and Mike Kenney, Harrier pilots. Tierney, thirty-eight, is wiry and intense. His call sign is "E.T." Kenney is younger and a little more jaunty. His call sign is "Pisser." He was awarded that name for his ability, after twenty-four hours of preparation, to urinate in an arc clear over a delivery truck.

Both men wear flight suits like Mad Dog's, and they are festooned with additional gear: G-suits, torso harnesses that will keep them securely strapped to their ejection seats, and floatation vests.

Finally the flight deck clears. E.T. and Pisser scramble up into their cockpits (right foot up stirrup-high to a fold-out step, left foot up on the jet engine intake, right foot up to the next step, and vault into the cockpit). They pull on desert-camouflage helmets, jam their sleeves up to midforearm, and start running through long checklists.

The Harrier is a small, single-seat aircraft. It is the only jet in the U.S. inventory that can take off from the deck of a ship on its own power (F14 Tomcats and F/A-18 Hornets are hurled off the decks of supercarriers by steam catapults). The Harrier's single engine, built by Rolls-Royce, develops enough thrust to blow seven tons of bricks from Virginia to California. That power is funneled behind the engine and vented out through four movable nozzles on the Harrier's belly. The nozzles are controlled from the cockpit.

If the nozzles are pointed straight down, the Harrier will go straight up (for every action, there is an equal and opposite reaction). If the nozzles are pointed downward at forty-five degrees, the Harrier will climb upward at forty-five degrees, or, given its weight of six and a half tons, something less than forty-five degrees.

The Harrier's directional nozzles give the airplane a characteristic highly irritating to enemy gunners. It can stop and hover in midair, and it can turn on a dime.

There's one other trick to this airplane. Along with aviation fuel, it

Dustin Sullenger helps strap in Dave Tierney.

carries a sizable tank of water. When Dave Tierney needs a great deal of power from his engine, he will inject water into the red-hot exhaust pipes. It is like pouring ice water on a sauna heater. The superheated steam will add many thousands of pounds of thrust—power—to the engine.

At present, Tierney has his nozzles pointed straight down, but he is throttled back enough so that his Harrier is perched comfortably on the flight deck. Now he reaches back, grabs the Plexiglas canopy, and shoves it forward. It closes with the solid sound of a Cadillac door. He communicates with Yellow Shirt with hand signals. Yellow Shirt holds up one hand, finger extended upward. He waggles the finger in the air. Tierney pushes forward the throttle and runs the engine up. The roar rattles the *Wasp* and echoes out over miles of ocean. Tierney doesn't give it anywhere near enough power to soar away, just enough to check the engine and make sure nothing is leaking.

Now Tierney swivels the nozzles to ten degrees down from horizontal and releases the brakes gingerly. His gray Harrier taxis out to the center of the flight deck, turns, and faces the bow some six hundred feet away. Beneath the plane's nose is a broad yellow stripe painted on the deck, marking the center of the deck and the line Tierney will follow on takeoff.

All systems checked, he is ready. Yellow Shirt signals him to run up the engine. Again a roar echoes across the water. The deckhands, all well behind the safety line, watch through their goggles. The air is filled with thunder and exhaust and vibration. If the deckhands weren't braced and holding on, they would be blasted overboard. Yellow Shirt waits for a thumbs up from Tierney. He gets a go-ahead from the tower. He waves five fingers at Tierney. Tierney pushes the throttle as far forward as it will go. Yellow Shirt then kneels and touches the deck in a good-bye salute.

The Harrier strains against its brakes. Tierney's helmet is hard against his headrest. The ship seems to hold its breath. Once Tierney heads down the yellow stripe, he either flies or he crashes. There is no place to abort a takeoff. If he hurtles off the end of the deck without enough power to fly, he will have milliseconds to eject from the Harrier before it hits the water. The danger is not that he will be trapped inside a sinking airplane. It is more immediate than that. The instant the Harrier hits the water, the impact will rip out the huge, red-hot engine (still at full throttle!) and shove it forward through Dave Tierney's back. He would

Harrier handlers.

have to depart before that happened. It is a slight occupational hazard, requiring good reflexes.

Tierney holds the brakes until the Harrier starts to skid down the deck. The engine is literally blowing him overboard. Tierney releases the brakes. He is committed. The blurred faces of the deckhands fly past. The tower flies past. The yellow line whips beneath the Harrier's nose. Tierney's eyes flicker between the yellow line he is steering and the instruments showing he has a good engine burn. One hand is poised above the nozzle direction lever. There is a slight bump as his wheels leave the end of the flight deck. The thunder and vibration drop away. Tierney slams the nozzle lever forward. Beneath the plane, the nozzles turn from level to fifty degrees down. The Harrier heads up.

"Thunder five five is airborne as fragged."

Tierney speaks into his radio, using the term for "scheduled."

"Roger that," says the tower as Tierney sets his nozzles straight back and carves a thundering arc into the sky. Pisser comes right behind him.

Soon they are back. Heads swivel as Tierney and Pisser rocket past the *Wasp* and sweep around to a position just off the port side rear of the flight deck. Yellow Shirt directs Tierney first. The Harrier, hovering with its nozzles pointed straight down, slides in over the flight deck and pauses. The deckhands brace.

It is a delicate moment. The maneuver calls for maximum engine power to keep the Harrier from crashing down. Tierney is sitting literally on a column of hot air, an inherently unstable place to be, and particularly because the sea breeze is gusting and the deck of the *Wasp* is slowly pitching and rolling fifty feet below him.

Tierney departs.

Tierney at altitude.

On the control panel in front of Tierney is a switch called the engine temperature limiter switch. It is on. If Tierney tries to hover heavy, laden with fuel or bombs, the engine will labor until it gets too hot. Then the limiter will automatically throttle back and Tierney will crash. In emergencies, Tierney can turn the switch off, allowing him to keep the throttle wide open. The engine will pour out power until it melts.

No need this time. Tierney comes in light, his limiter switch on. He is injecting water. Twenty-one thousand pounds of thrust is beating on the half-inch steel plate of the flight deck. On the other side of this steel plate is Gunny Porter. Porter is the MEU's administrator and is working on pay vouchers. A gremlin has placed his office, out of the thousands of places on the ship, directly beneath the Harriers' landing zone. Inside Porter's tiny cubbyhole, the noise is deafening. If somebody screamed in his ear, he'd never hear it. Might not even feel it.

Yellow Shirt directs Tierney down gently. The six-ton airplane hits the deck at about the speed of a boy leaping down a flight of six stairs.

Tierney and Mike Kenney come home.

Below, Porter grimaces and goes back to work. Tierney taxis away as Pisser comes in to hover and land.

As activity subsides on the flight deck, a welcome announcement comes to the Marines confined below decks. "The ship is secured from flight quarters," the 1MC booms. "The flight deck is open for PT."

Marines pour out of hatches and scramble up onto the flight deck for free-time PT, or physical training. It has been another in a long series of long days. Lejeune is weeks behind; Somalia, or whever they're going, is weeks ahead.

For Marines like Danny Fish and Mad Dog and Dave Tierney, these are fifteen- or twenty-hour days with not enough time to get everything done. For the ground combat Marines, the float has already sailed past ennui and tedium into paralyzing boredom. The taped TV shows and movies (*Maverick . . . Leave It to Beaver . . .* Wrestlemania VIII . . . *Superman*) are starting to come around for the second time. The only news is the *Wasp Wing*, a one-sheet compliation of recent crime and sports news abridged into two- and three-sentence stories. Magazines that arrived with the last mail (*Car & Driver, Golf Magazine, Triathlete Magazine, Ameri-*

can Rifleman) are limp and dog-eared with use. In the officers' lounge, pilots huddle over a game of Risk.

The MEU's youngest officers, its lieutenants, have organized a competition to see who can go the longest without spanking the monkey (masturbating). A renegade group has started a countercompetition: who can record the greatest number of successful spankings within a twenty-four-hour period. Some enlisted Marines have discovered how to turn off the air-conditioning, or the toilet flush water, up in officers' country. A playful skirmish of sabotage and countersabotage is breaking out.

Staff Sergeant North is in a foul mood after weeks of no mail. As he passes the ship's post office on his way back from chow, he bangs on the window grille.

"Where's my mail?" he demands with a stern face.

Inside, a young squid postal clerk has learned to cower when North's face appears. He thinks North is joking. But he's not sure. North, after all, is a Marine, a trained killer. Probably has a weapon stashed away somewhere. No telling what that boy might do.

North knows there will be no mail until the ship reaches the Mediterranean in a week or so. But he has learned to cherish this small diversion.

Harrier ground crew.

Jose Rocha.

Enlisted head. From left, Jarvis Goggins, Ronnie Smith, Stephen Gray, Marlin Williams. Background: Dan Bill.

Officers' lounge.

"Hey! Where's my fuckin' mail?" he bellows at the terrified clerk every time he passes, which is several times a day.

"I'm just fuckin' with 'im," he says with a grin.

Down in enlisted berthing, a couple of Marines are taunting Eddie Adams with a skin magazine. "Look, she's beautiful," one Marine says. "What's wrong with worshipping the Lord's work?"

It begins to wear on people after a while—the practical jokes, the boredom, the almost total lack of privacy, the constant noise, the same old faces, same old food, same old routine, and months yet to go. It amplifies the stresses they are already under: trying to master their jobs, worrying about their families back home, many of them wondering if their lady will stay as true as she promised the night before the MEU shipped out.

A Marine officer is talking into the wall phone in the officers' lounge. "How many airplanes do we have up right now? Three? That's fucking shit! . . . Who said that? Well, people are sticking their decisions all over the place. Everything's a priority, right? Well, everything can't *be* a fucking priority!" He slams the phone back into its cradle and stalks off.

"A lot of these guys are walking pressure cookers," says Father William Devine, the *Wasp*'s chaplain. A Roman Catholic priest with a sharp Boston twang, Devine is an informal kind of guy beloved by Marines. (In a fit of religious passion during a sermon to Marines, he once cried out, "God really . . . gives a *shit* about you men!")

"A lot of them come down here to talk, somebody's been yelling at them, they're busting their ass and . . . it just gets too much," Devine says in his tiny office aboard the *Wasp*.

"Many a guy I have just held in my arms," he adds.

"A lot of them come from dysfunctional families; the military gives them the discipline and the responsibility and the commitment. The military gives them values. It's almost a sense of family, bound together by responsibility and commitment to each other and yes, affection. . . .

"These kids get a lot more out of the military than the GI bill," says Devine.

Now the late afternoon sun beats down on the rough tarred surface of the flight deck. The sun, the salt air, the gusting wind are invigorating. Marines in shorts are pounding around the flight deck. Fenton goes by, then North. Rocha and Adams. McGuffee has the *Ragin' Cajun* pulled out

Eddie Adams, at *Wasp* chapel.

Eddie Adams.

Trash dump.

of line for maintenance; he is high atop a rotor head, working with his flight suit stripped to his waist. The jogging Marines sweep around the helo and head on down toward the Harriers, turn, and struggle against the wind up toward the bow. Four turns on the flight deck is a mile.

After an hour, most Marines flop down on the deck to doze or watch the sea. Steve McGowin, a sergeant who works in the intelligence shop, writes a letter to his teenage son and daughter, reminding them of his rules for dating: (1) Parents own the clock. If they say home by eleven, they mean eleven, not ten after. (2) No riding in a car driven by anyone who's had a drop of alcohol. Ever. Call home and someone'll pick you up. (3) Don't get in a position where you are encouraged to use narcotics. (4) Don't get in a position where you are forced to become a parent.

McGowin used to be a cop in Andalusia, Ala., doing drug busts. His wife Cathy made him get out of that business because it was too dangerous. Now he's a Marine on his way to Somalia. He finishes his letter and stares out at the setting sun, worrying about Cathy and the kids.

Sitting next to him, dangling his long legs over the edge of the flight deck, is Eddie Adams. Eddie's daddy was a guitar picker and bluegrass singer, and he died when Eddie was fourteen. Eddie stayed away from school a whole year. He finally managed to graduate and drifted into the Marines, attracted by the hard life, the camaraderie and discipline. He ran with a hard-drinking, womanizing crowd. He eventually washed up in a Marine Corps prison, busted, broke, alone, and desperate. "I hurt inside all the time," he says. "I just wanted somebody to hold me." He thought seriously about suicide. It was about that time that another Marine "started witnessing to me, introducing me to Jesus."

In the years since, Eddie has become a devout born-again Christian. Although he loves being a Marine, he was deeply worried about coming on this float. "I am not at all afraid of battle," he says. "That's what we're here for. What I am afraid of is staying true against the vulgarity of living on the ship. I am tempted by pornography. Many of the things I believe in the other guys don't believe. It's just ignorance. And when I try to talk about Jesus they just think I'm tryin' to be better than them. I say no—I'm a sinner like you," he says with a broad grin.

Eddie is learning he can be tough. His religious convictions and evangelical calling are being tempered, hardened, and polished, by enlisted berthing. "Loving God is not Bible thumping," he says up on the flight deck. "It's, you need something done? I'll do it. Need ten dollars? Here, take it. This is total faith."

As the *Wasp* plods along in an empty sea, dozens of brown paper trash bags suddenly sail through the air and plop into the water, bobbing gently astern. It is the day's trash and garbage, tossed overboard every evening. "That's unsat [unsatisfactory], man," says a Marine watching the stuff bob away. "Gotta be a better way."

Down a bit from Eddie Adams is Chris Baron. Chris is half listening to other Marines talking about their wives and girlfriends. Chris's life is a little empty. He is twenty-three, and he is starting to get serious about settling down. Maybe having kids. The wind and waves lull him into a fantasy. . . .

"Attention on the flight deck!" bawls the 1MC. "The flight deck is secured from PT. All hands stand clear of the flight deck! The flight deck is secured from PT!"

Flight deck, sunset.

Chris Baron and Eddie Adams and Steve McGowin and other Marines and sailors heave themselves to their feet and begin filing below deck. Each takes a last look at the pink glow fading from the western sky back toward Camp Lejeune. Ahead, the sky is jet black. The wind is picking up. It blusters across the flight deck and twists and tumbles through the helicopter rotor blades tied down to the deck. The blades thrum and shrill in the windy darkness, sounding like distant shrieks of agony and despair.

An hour later, Father William Devine, *Wasp*'s chaplain, comes on the 1MC with the evening prayer.

"Help us to work well with each other," he says in his nasal Boston twang. "Help us to realize that our safety and success depend not solely on what we do, but on thy grace. . . . Help us to get home safely, O Lord. Amen."

QUESTION: Do you think you work harder, for longer hours, than most American civilians?

Some days, yes. Like field ops, combat, etc. Then some days we don't do a thing all day and I actually feel guilty at payday.
—Sergeant, Infantry

Absolutely longer. Not always harder. Flying isn't work.
—Captain, Cobra Attack Helicopter Pilot

6

TARGET TOWN
SOUTHERN SOMALIA
March 1993

As the *Wasp* steams off the southern Somali coastline, Broderick assembles his staff for a brainstorming session in the Flag Plot. This is a small room, perhaps two-thirds the size of a typical Holiday Inn room. It is called the Flag Plot because it was built for admirals ("flags") to lay out their battle maps and charts and plot the battle.

Flag Plot sits inside the *Wasp*'s nerve center. Here is the ship's Combat Information Center, a darkened space cluttered with radar screens and computer terminals where naval officers monitor external threats to the ship (incoming missiles, small-boat or aircraft attack) and can direct the counterattack. Next door is the Marines' command center, where Marines monitor and direct their operations.

The command complex, built into the center of the ship to minimize the potential for being knocked out in an attack, is reached through a long, narrow passageway that runs down the center of the ship just below the flight deck. Like other passageways, it is studded with watertight bulkheads. To get through, Marines rotate a long steel lever, pull open the door, step over a ten-inch-high doorjamb, pull the door closed behind them and dog down the lever. A constant "squeak . . . thump . . . squeak" echoes through the ship as people bustle up and down the passageway. "When I get home, I'm gonna go around leaving all the doors open," says an irritated Marine.

The passageway ends abruptly at a heavy metal door. On the wall beside the steel door is four-key electronic pad. Access is gained by punching in the correct code. The code is 4-3-2-1.

Inside, a long conference table covered in green felt has been squeezed into the Flag Plot, barely leaving room for two dozen metal chairs. All of them are filled with Marines. The miracle of air-conditioning has chilled the Flag Plot below sixty degrees, but no one complains and the Marines wear their sleeves rolled up tight over their biceps in prescribed hot-weather fashion.

It is late March, a few days after the return of the convoy from Doobhley (enlisted Marines refer to that operation as the "Doobhley Death March"). Broderick has spread a map out over the table and is stabbing repeatedly at a point near the crease. It is the southern Somali town of Afmadow. The town is where two major gunrunning routes converge. If the warlords are secretly drawing their weapons out of their UN-authorized storage caches and and taking them elsewhere, the guns have to come through Afmadow.

"These are the guys who say they don't want Americans in their

Broderick, Flag Plot.

area," says Broderick. "So that's where I wanna go. I wanna do a helluva assault into Afmadow, sweep right through the town, get right in their faces.

"They're saying, don't come in or we'll shoot. Well, that's a helluva attitude. I'm thinking of a reinforced rifle company. Whaddya think?"

Broderick's brainstorming sessions are just that. There is no formality here. If someone has a better idea, he is encouraged to voice it. (Broderick doesn't just listen to his officers; he makes a point of regularly touring the ship and talking to grunts. If the inertial navigation systems on the Harriers are going haywire, Broderick often will know about it from the mechanics before his air officer does. If Jon Flores has a better idea for keeping the Hell Bitch's fuel filter clean, Broderick hears it.)

In Flag Plot, Broderick calls his captains and majors by their first names. Each is a recognized expert in his field. Mark Toal, commander of Charlie Company, knows what his men can do and what they can't do. George Fenton, Broderick's operations officer, can spot a Murphy in a plan from a mile away.

Broderick's officers call the colonel by his first name, too. Sir.

Among those who speak up is Joel McBroom.

He is a round-faced captain who commands the MEU's Weapons Company. His men have ten souped-up WWII-type Jeeps, painted black and mounted with antitank missiles or heavy machine guns. They are called Fast Attack Vehicles. The MEU has been off the Somali coast nine days. McBroom's men haven't been off the ship yet. They are itching for action. So is McBroom.

"Sir, ah, if they've got heavy weapons up there we could be out-gunned," McBroom says, hoping Broderick will put his Weapons Company into the operation.

No luck.

"I disagree," says Broderick. "We have Cobras to deal with the heavy stuff," he says, referring to his missile-firing helicopter gunships.

Broderick gets up to leave. "Get your brains crackin' on this," he says over his shoulder.

When he's gone, someone says, "I know what the colonel said, but I think we're gonna need more firepower up there. If we've got vehicles fleeing out of the town, we might have a problem."

The Cobras can deal with trucks, says another officer. "The problem is on-station time. They can't loiter all that long."

As the Marine officers wrestle with the problem, a certain amount of frustration is evident. When they were training for Somalia four months ago at Camp Lejeune, they, too, had seen the horrifying TV pictures of starving humanity. They arrived here in Somalia with a blinding ambition to help, stepping confidently into this cesspool of meanness and misery with soaring spirits: We're tough professionals. We can deal with the warlords. We're Americans—we can help. We can fix Somalia.

But it is quickly becoming evident that Somalia will not yield so easily to American "can-do" enthusiasm. Broderick and his Marines are professionals at the business of military operations. They are very, very good. They know how to assault Afmadow. But what then?

The question worries several of Broderick's top staff officers. Who is watching the next town over? Who's watching the gunrunners' routes two hundred miles away? And what's the point, anyway? If the warlords are allowed to keep their weapons, won't they just wait until the Americans go away before starting the war again?

The consensus among these officers is that there doesn't seem to be a coherent military plan to subdue the warlords and impose peace on the countryside.

And that's not all. Even if there were a coherent military plan, there is no broader political strategy to fit it into. There's no reason to assault Afmadow—no reason to risk American and Somali lives—if there is no larger purpose.

In Washington, the strategy—insofar as anyone is still paying attention to Somalia—is to bring all U.S. troops home and turn the mess over to the United Nations (the U.S. troops that had been sent here in December were supposed to be home two months ago). The UN is still struggling to assemble the peacekeeping forces with which it will run the country as of May 2, 1993, the day the United States turns responsibility over to the UN. The UN hasn't got the time, or the staff, for long-range planning.

"What we ought to be doing is analyzing the bases of the warlords' power and systematically setting out to destroy those bases," says one of Broderick's senior officer.

"They get income and power from providing security for UN food shipments and from the khat [narcotic leaf] trade. Get them out of those businesses. Then, we should have a long-term presence. Give each Marine unit a manageable area and keep them out there on the streets. Have the UN diplomats working on rebuilding the political structure and your military forces providing security, and you could—over time—begin to turn things around," this officer says.

Instead, Broderick's orders seem to be: See what you can do. Do a little patrolling, a little humanitarian stuff. No decisive engagement. Try to stay neutral in the shifting quicksand of Somali politics. Do what you can to get Somalia "back on its feet," a phrase used routinely by senior U.S. officials who have not defined precisely what that means.

It is not a noble mission. Whatever hope and glory (and press coverage) attended the first landing of the Marines in Somalia in December 1992 has long since been ground away by the relentless heat and hopelessness of Somalia. "A lot of Somalis just deserve to be killed," says a senior U.S. commander in a moment of bitter candor. The sentiment is shared by many missionaries and relief workers who see their clinics looted, farm projects wiped out, volunteer nurses shot.

American and UN military officers in Mogadishu, scrambling to devise a strategy to deal with the mess the politicians have left them, have begun using the Vietnam War phrase, "winning hearts and minds" (WHAM), to describe efforts to bring peace to this tortured land.

Broderick has assigned 123 of his Marines to patrol duty in Mogadishu. They are out in force day and night, braving the occasional snipers, making friends on the street, handing out soccer balls and red USMC T-shirts to kids who seem friendly. Keeping a fragile, armed peace.

"Machine guns and lollipops," says a Marine general approvingly.

But a grimmer reality is recorded by the grunts.

"You can't trust the kids," Ernesto Garcia tells his buddies as he returned to the *Wasp* from a week on patrol in Mogadishu. "They make you feel sorry for them. During the day they beg for food, then at night they come at you with guns. You can never let yourself soften up and feel for them," he said. Lance Corporal Garcia, from San Antonio, Tex., is twenty-one.

Here in southern Somalia, Broderick has sought permission to transport grain to some outlying villages where food supplies are rare. Permission denied; that's the job of the relief agencies. The warlords still have their weapons, cached in towns like Doobhley. They can't be inspected or destroyed; that's UN policy.

What Broderick is left with is the constant threat and sputtering violence of a civil war waged on the cheap. In the towns and cities are crowds

of people, poor but not starving. There are many idle young men who may or may not be clan soldiers, and children and elders who may or may not be hiding old rifles or AK-47s under their skirts. A couple of land mines may be hidden under a dirty blanket, waiting for a moment of revenge. A market woman may be carrying a hand grenade or two in the basket atop her head.

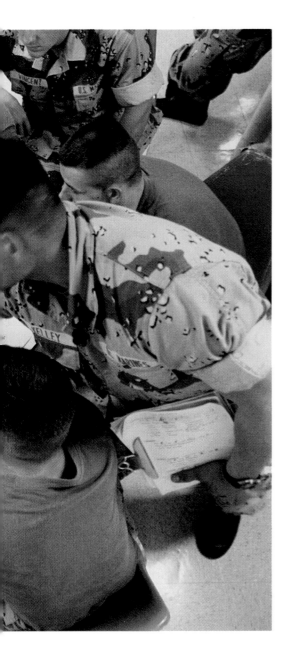

Ops planning.

It is a nasty puzzle, and the politicians and TV commentators who caused Broderick and his men to be here are far away. It is no longer their responsibility.

As Broderick's plan to assault Afmadow takes shape, he decides to send McBroom ashore to get the local intelligence, or "gouge," from the Belgian commanders.

Elated, McBroom goes back to the cramped stateroom he shares with Mark Toal to get his gear. Toal is working at his tiny desk. He has been assigned as the ground force commander for the raid into Afmadow. He has already put his men to work on thrashing out lists of gear, cleaning weapons, and thinking about tactics. This evening, a helo will fly Toal over Afmadow on a visual reconnaissance. When he returns he will start drawing up plans for the operation, analyzing the terrain, likely weather, time and space constraints, and logistics.

Won't the gunrunners in Afmadow be tipped off by a helo circling overhead? Toal looks up. "That's always a consideration," he says.

Down in the echoing hangar deck, one of Toal's staff sergeants, Joseph Dunn, is briefing his platoon. "We're looking at doing another op in the next forty-eight hours," he says.

"Yee-*hah!*" his men yell, giving each other high fives.

"We don't know if or when this is gonna happen," Dunn continues as his men gather around him. "There's a lot of anti-American people up there. But I don't want you guys stressing out until we know what's there and if we're going."

Lieutenant Doug McIntyre is also briefing his men on the hangar deck. He has laid out white tape on the deck in the approximate shape of several huts, outlining walls and doorways. "Okay, we're gonna sweep this village, there's not going to be shooting in the area, but we have to defend ourselves and take them out if we need to. You're gonna have plenty of ammunition."

Soon, McIntyre has his men in rehearsal. They trot holding their rifles with both hands, pointed down. They pause at a "doorway."

"Fonce goin' in!" yells Antonio Fonce, a twenty-two-year-old from El Paso. He ducks into the doorway.

"Fonce comin' out!"

The point is to use shock and speed to overwhelm any resistance, McIntyre explains. Always yell out your location so your buddy doesn't shoot you by accident. Watch for booby traps.

"This is the most casualty-producing type of combat there is," says McIntyre, twenty-six.

Up in Toal's stateroom, meanwhile, the phone has rung with a message for McBroom. He is not to go ashore for liaison with the Belgians; someone else is going. Instead, McBroom is to prepare to take the Hell Bitch and six other light armored vehicles (LAVs) on the raid to Afmadow.

Toal is still working on his maps and charts. His main concern is potential armed opposition. There are thirty-five hundred people in Afmadow. It is not known how many carry weapons. The LAVs will help; they can carry six Marines and a 25-mm automatic chain gun firing two hundred rounds a minute. Toal cheers himself up thinking of having the LAVs.

Then the phone rings again. The LAV part of the raid is "canked," or canceled, because of the threat of land mines. McBroom's face gets beet red. He throws the map on his rack.

"Okaaaay, change number fucking eight!" he says.

The next afternoon the MEU staff gathers for a lengthy confirmation brief, to discuss and refine the plan for Afmadow. Two photo enlargements of Afmadow, taken during last night's recon mission, are propped up on easels at the front of the wardroom. Vegetation and open areas are marked in color, and critical sites are marked.

Colonel Fenton leads the meeting at a brusque clip. "Two?"

Larry Hamilton, the MEU's intelligence officer (S-2), gets to his feet and gives a precise, detailed briefing on Afmadow's political and military situation.

"The town itself has been victimized by both sides. Plundered. Last month Special Forces guys got a cordial welcome, but they went in this month and had to leave quickly because of threats of physical violence. The people in Afmadow don't know we're coming. They will be a little scared, startled at first, and they sometimes do stupid things. There is no formal government. There is a council of elders."

Okay, says Fenton. "S-1 we heard from, S-2 we heard, S-3, nothing. . . . Legal?"

The MEU legal officer rises. "Sir. You can't go into houses and search unless there is reasonable evidence there are weapons there. We are looking for illegal weapons caches, not individual weapons. Conduct: treat these houses like they were your mother's home, with respect. I recommend we release all detainees at the conclusion of the search."

"Unless they shoot at Marines," Broderick interjects. He is making a small pile of splintered Rite-Aid toothpicks.

Now Mark Toal rises to brief his plan.

He will take in 275 people in twenty-one "sticks": most of Charlie Company, reinforced with Marines from Weapons Company, engineers and other specialists, and sixty Belgian troops. Eleven helos will ferry the teams in two waves; the helos of each wave will descend on Afmadow simultaneously. First wave will hit the landing zone, or LZ, at 0630. LZs are labeled Snipe, Eagle, Wren, and Robin.

McBroom's Fast Attack Vehicles have been put back in the plan; they will zoom around providing security, responding to emergencies and transporting the wounded, if any. Five of Toal's platoons will stage near the town center, then spread out and sweep the town for weapons. For coordination purposes, Toal has divided the town into sectors separated by lines designated Phase Line Michelob, Phase Line Heineken, Phase Line Schlitz.

Toal uses his pointer to indicate the LZs. "The mosque is a target reference," he says. "It is not a target, it is a no-fire, no-search area. Command post at the old police station, here. I'm setting up the medical guys at the old Red Crescent hospital, here."

Broderick has ordered a team of doctors and medics to accompany Toal into Afmadow. They will set up a medical clinic for the townspeople while the search is under way. Machine guns and lollipops.

Broderick: "That LZ you got there is kinda close to the hospital. We're gonna have people lying on the dirt floor, we don't wanna blow more dirt all over 'em."

"Roger that, sir," says Toal. The LZ will be located farther away.

Toal continues. "The searches will be nonaggressive. We're not gonna be knocking down doors unless that's okay with the elders. Mine-detection teams will be out with us. If we find ordnance we have C4 [plastic explosive] to blow it."

Helos will begin extracting the force at 1400. Snipers will be stationed at the LZ. "If there are missing Marines, we don't plan on leaving without them," says Toal.

"You'll hold the whole force?" asks Broderick.

"If I have to, sir," says Toal.

"Maybe just leave forty guys and the Cobras until you round 'em up," says Broderick.

"Roger that, sir."

The meeting veers off into a discussion of the weapons search itself, the whole point of this operation. Do the Marines have the right to search every house, or only where they suspect weapons are hidden? Do they have to ask someone's permission, and if they do, would a gunman hiding a dozen weapons give it?

"You must have evidence there are weapons there before you go in," insists Broderick's legal officer.

"You should have 'reasonable cause,' not 'probable cause,'" says another officer. "Probable cause is too high a standard."

The officers settle on "reasonable."

If the raid force is met with hostility and shooting, Toal's plan is for his men to sweep the town anyway. If hostile crowds gather, Toal will call in two of the giant CH-53 helos to hover at fifteen feet. The gale-force downdraft will disperse them.

"Or," says Broderick, "bring in the Cobras and blow their asses all over the street."

What do you do, Broderick wonders aloud, when a bunch of Somali women start throwing rocks, like they do in Mogadishu?

Here is a serious problem, one that plagues the Marines and other U.S. forces in Somalia in the spring of 1993. Looking tough and acting friendly is a delicate balance. Rock throwers threaten to upset that balance. A rock-throwing mob can easily get out of hand. And in Somalia, a charging mob of rock throwers often conceals a second wave of armed sharpshooters.

So the Marines must use enough force to get the job done and to protect themselves, but not enough to incite wider violence and needless death. Each man must be able, under extreme stress, to instantly recognize the difference. The Marines are heavily armed, but every time they shoot, a command investigation will take place. Two Marines who arrived in Somalia the previous December were court martialed on weapons charges (one was convicted, the other acquitted).

The rule is "proportionate force." Toal says later, "This New World Order stuff is putting a huge new responsibility on these kids—huge. It's hard enough for somebody with a college education and years of experience to explain proportionate force. But for a nineteen-year-old kid who's never been out of the country, in a high-stress situation where he's getting rocks thrown at him and the guns are behind the rock throwers, what is 'proportionate'?"

There is another, darker, consideration lurking behind the discussion. Crudely put, how many lives is this mission worth? Sure, the Marines have volunteered to put their lives on the line. But to needlessly sacrifice them is a mortal sin as great as any commander can imagine.

Out here in Somalia, there is no magic formula to determine the lev-

Ops planning.

els of risk, to balance out the goals of U.S. foreign policy with the lives of
Mark Toal and Eddie Adams and Jose Rocha. No one at the White House
or Pentagon or in Congress has to make that judgment. Instead, it falls on
the commanders here. Broderick and his staff, ground commanders like
Toal, on down to platoon sergeants and fire-team leaders who will make
snap decisions on the ground.

"You gotta beat yourself up early on this question, is it worth the risk,
and at what point am I willing to take casualties," says Truman "Butch"
Preston, the MEU's executive officer. Lieutenant Colonel Preston, short
and bald, has had plenty of experience doing just that. A special-operations
officer, he has spent most of his career on overseas operations rather than
driving a desk at headquarters.

"You have to know your people real well, what they're capable of
doing and what they can't do," Preston says. "When you exceed their skill
levels, you're hanging yourself out there. I don't get hung up on the political ramifications. Sometimes you just have to say, it's worth the risk. People get paid to make those judgments. And they have to live with it."

Meanwhile, Broderick is still worrying about rock-throwing women in Afmadow.

"The helos will hold 'em only so long," he tells the meeting. "Let's start thinking about this. Shit, I dunno. Maybe we have our own rock throwers come up and throw the damn things back. . . . If it gets bad, I'll fly in CS [tear gas] and smoke the whole goddamn place."

One other point. Broderick has been racking his brain to find something positive he can do for the people of Afmadow. Hearts and minds. He has ceremonial plaques and souvenir *Wasp* hats to hand out to visiting dignitaries, but nothing for kids. What he comes up with are 3M Post-it note pads and ballpoint pens.

"I can't go around saving the world—I don't have the supplies to do it," he explains. "But my guys are Americans. They have big hearts and they want to help." He shrugs. "You do what you can."

George Fenton whips along a MEU briefing.

Truman "Butch" Preston.

The meeting breaks up on that note. Toal goes back to his stateroom to finalize his helo loading plan. It is late evening. The Afmadow raid will launch in seven hours. He is working at his tiny desk when the door bursts open. It is one of the pilots with bad news. The *Wasp* has been asked to fly two warlords to a peace conference. All of the ship's helos will be in use tomorrow. If one bird malfunctions, it will wreck the plan Toal has worked out to fly everyone out of Afmadow tomorrow afternoon.

"Okay," says Toal, "I guess the word is, stay flexible."

"It's all gonna come together, buddy," says the aviator. "Good luck."

0415. Eddie Adams hits the deck. Around him in the eerie red glow of the *Wasp*'s night lighting, men are rushing about, pulling on fatigues, stuffing feet into boots, twisting into flak jackets. Adams buckles on his deuce gear, feels for his ammo pouches, canteens, and first aid pack, and joins the stream of men pouring out the door and down the steps toward the hangar deck.

Grunting and cursing, they struggle through hatches and down the

Flight deck ramp.

narrow passageways. The hangar deck is already hot, with a damp breeze sighing in from the blackness outside the elevator doors. Adams finds his platoon and a space on the floor. He lies down, knees up, his weapon cradled in his lap. His weapon is a lightweight (twenty-pound) machine gun. Around him Marines are loading pallets of ammo and MREs and water to go in with them on the helos. Above, Mad Dog is firing up the *Ragin' Cajun*, parked with seven other CH-46 helos nose to tail along the flight deck. The noise drifts down through the open doors, mixed with the moist predawn air, exhaust fumes, and the smell of adrenaline.

"Lotta people got bad feelings about this," says Zach Bower, a twenty-one-year-old rifleman from Roanoke, Va. "I think we'll find some weapons, but they know we're coming. They're not stupid. I think it's gonna be real dangerous."

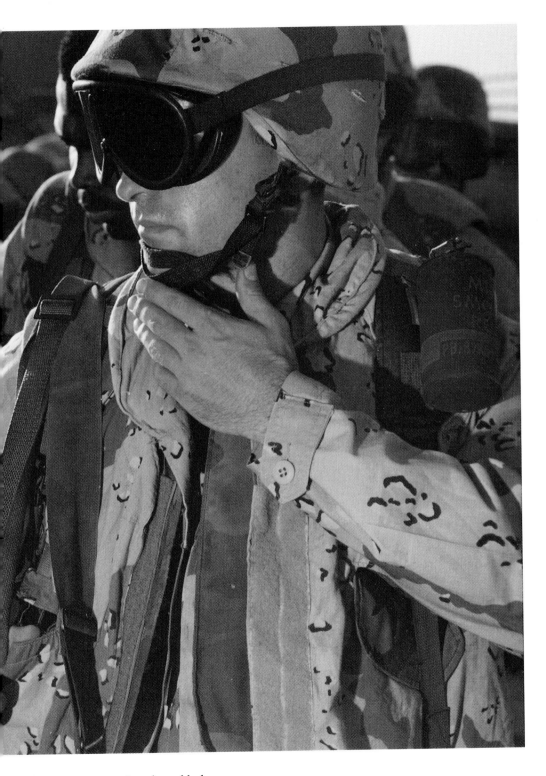

Marines wait to board helo.

At 0530, dawn begins to lighten the sky outside. Marines have been staged on the hangar deck for sixty minutes. At 0630 sudden shouts rouse them. They stand up and shuffle off to the interior ramp leading up to the flight deck. There, they halt again, jammed together in the hot darkness. Most Marines try to sit on the sharply sloped ramp.

"The adrenaline has no place to go, you just sit and absorb it into your skin," says a Marine morosely.

At 0725 the waiting Marines are roused again. A crashing din of stinking hot exhaust hits them as they sprint across the rough tarred flight deck. They duck beneath the whirling blades and clamber up the rear ramps of the six helos waiting at the edge of a bloodred sea. Mad Dog watches in his rearview mirror as the men scramble into the frayed red canvas seats along the fuselage. They buckle their seat belts, lean back, and place their rifles point down between their knees among a pile of water cans, medical packs, stretchers, radios, and a few machine guns. Jiggling like marionettes, they assume the suffering, vacant stares of riders on the New York City subway.

Jose Rocha, twenty-four, and Steve Conway, twenty-two, allow their eyes to wander over the spaghetti tangle of wires and tubes exposed on the interior of the shaking aircraft. It was built in 1969, twenty-four years ago. Like most grunts, Rocha and Conway are extremely wary of helos. They're land magnets, man. Everybody knows somebody who's gone down in one. Some have had close shaves themselves.

Conway remembers banking off the deck in a Frog like this one, but instead of seeing the flight deck get smaller beneath him, Conway saw it float up above his window. Next, he saw the hangar deck doors rise past his window. "The crew chief came running back swearing, and banged a pipe a couple of times, and we went up," says Conway. "Guess it wasn't our turn."

Rocha recalls an old hand once telling him, if you get on a helo and the hydraulic lines aren't leaking on you, get out fast—something's wrong.

Now, as Mad Dog massages his controls and the helo lurches off the deck, a liquid drop forms on a shaking tube and splats at Rocha's feet. Under his helmet and goggles, Rocha gives a tight smile.

Eighteen minutes later, Mad Dog starts yanking and banking. None of the previous flights has reported taking fire here, but you never know.

Mad Dog will go in fast. The Marines studiously watch their feet as the horizon gyrates past the windows. Then the ground straightens out and races beneath them. Mad Dog flares the nose high and touches down. The rear ramp is already dropping. Marines sprint out into the bright sunlight and across a stony field, eddying up against a broken stone wall, weapons ready. Mad Dog is disappearing toward the horizon. Silence descends.

The Marines are pumped for combat. Aboard the *Wasp* last night, Dunn and the other platoon sergeants passed the word: This is Indian country. This is real-world. Be careful.

The Marines have drawn thousands of rounds of ammunition. They are authorized to use force to respond to an "immediate hostile act or hostile intent." Many have written last letters home.

Marines suffer a helo ride.

This is it. They quickly form up and start moving along a broad, baked-clay street into the center of town. It is oppressively hot. Knots of sullen Somalis watch silently. The Marines grip their weapons and walk, sweat trickling under their helmets and flak jackets, eyes flickering for any sign of hostile intent. Their heavy boots scrunch on the stones. Most of the Somalis are barefoot.

A Somali woman comes toward one Marine in the center of the street. She swishes purposively along in long, colorful robes, her head held proudly high, eyes straight ahead. The Marine nervously tries to re-

Afmadow.

call the Somali phrases he studied aboard ship last night. "Hello" is . . . "*Sa . . . sha . . . ?*" He swallows hard as she approaches.

"*Shalom*," he blurts as the woman passes.

At a crossroads in the center of town, Toal and Richard Natonski, the lieutenant colonel who commands the Marine infantry, are meeting with the town elders. They are gaunt and gnarled old men wearing loose, short-sleeve shirts, the traditional long skirts of dusty material tucked in at the waist, and plastic shower sandals. Natonski and Toal tower over them in their heavy boots, flak jackets, and helmets.

Afmadow elders.

Mark Toal.

"Tell them that I will personally tell the Big Boss that you need food," Natonski says through his translator. "Tell them we would like to show them the hospital where we will treat their people."

To Toal, Natonski remarks, "They're a little upset, they won't shake our hands. I told them we come in peace."

The elders blink in the hard sunlight. Cattle bawl in the distance. A pair of Harriers appears with a ripping sound and thunders overhead. Toal turns away to get a radio message from the LZ. Everyone's in safely.

"Nightstalker, Badger," he radios out to the *Wasp*. "Seahawks."

As Toal waits for acknowledgment, a purple butterfly lands on his backpack radio.

At the edge of town, two helos circle, on station to evacuate Marines if necessary. The heat rises in waves from the stony ground. Marines gulp warm water from their canteens. In the center of town are a few one-

Patrol, Afmadow.

story concrete buildings. They have no roofs or windows. Electric wires
dangle uselessly from a pole. Two white goats wander through the town
square. A donkey pulls a rusty fifty-gallon drum on a cart. A woman sits
on the ground, ignoring the newcomers. In a Stone Age ritual, she chaffs
wheat in a basket.

"We got no fucking business here," says Staff Sergeant North as he
plods along with his weapon.

The Marines turn up a rutted lane and begin their search, stepping
carefully through a low fence of brambles and into a neatly swept compound of houses constructed of sticks and mud. They knock on a flimsy
door. No answer.

"Cover my rear—one two three go!" shouts a Marine.

"Diaz in!" he yells as he ducks inside. A moment later, "Diaz coming
out!" and "Diaz out! All clear!"

As the sun climbs in the sky, the Marines search through the flimsy houses, pawing through each family's cooking pots and rags and precious bundles of belongings. Gaunt mothers gather screaming children to their skirts and hollow-eyed men watch with cold anger. Whatever careful rules that Broderick's staff has set down—"reasonable" cause or "probable" cause—are trampled in the heat and dust.

Sergeant Carl Chapman and his team of engineers sweep the town for land mines, using a magnetic detector on the end of a long pole. At the edge of town their detector needle starts jumping. They mark off a large mine field. Someday, maybe, someone will come and remove the mines.

Hut search, Afmadow.

The Marines find no weapons. They hand out their few Post-it pads and pens to some of the kids trotting along beside them. Soon there are throngs of children, shrieking and jabbering, reaching out for goodies and tugging at the Marines' canteens.

Irritated and sweltering, the Marines begin using the caustic slang of Vietnam, referring to the houses as "hootches," to the town as "the ville," and to Somalis as "gooks."

In one compound the Marines come across a child resting in the shade of a spreading thorn tree. He is a beautiful child. His dark liquid eyes are glazed with disease and pain. He sits perfectly still on a cowhide surrounded by his family, awaiting with dignity the release of death.

Jeremy LaChapelle and dying child.

"Hey—this kid's sick," says a Marine. The men come to a pause, panting in the blinding heat, staring down at the child.

Corporal Antonio Fonce squats and reaches out a hand of compassion toward the child. But he falters at an impenetrable barrier of culture and language and disease. Fonce is from El Paso. He is twenty-two.

"What's wrong with him?" Fonce pleadingly asks the child's mother. She glances at the aunts and uncles and elders gathered in the shade. They shrug helplessly at the foreign words.

"*Is he sick?*" Fonce asks. Shrug.

"Get a corpsman," someone says. "Get a translator."

A lance corporal is sent trotting off. Flies buzz in the profound African silence.

"Fuck 'em, let's move," a Marine says abruptly. "He's gonna die anyway. Nothin' we can do." The judgment stings. But after an embarrassed hesitation, most of the Marines move out. A corpsman is on the way. That is the most these Marines can do. They regroup and move on out toward Phase Line Michelob. A Harrier flashes overhead, and helicopters drone in the distance. Underneath the shade tree, the Somalis sit.

Soon, Jeremy LaChapelle arrives. He is a Navy corpsman attached to Charlie Company. He is thoroughly trained in battlefield first aid. But nothing in his medical training or in his upbringing in Rock, Mich., has prepared him to hold in his hands the life of this child sitting in the dust of Afmadow. LaChapelle is twenty years old.

Loosening the Velcro fasteners on his flak vest, he drops his corpsman's bag and squats in the dust, pulling on a pair of disposable rubber gloves. The child stares solemnly at him.

"Can he keep down liquids?" he asks the mother. She smiles. "Tell him to follow my fingers with his eyes," he says. She smiles. In desperation, he rummages through his kit for the help he knows is not there. The elders watch.

"C'mon, Doc, what's wrong with him?" asks a Marine.

LaChapelle gently wipes down the child's back, which has been slathered with a blackish goo. LaChapelle guesses it is some kind of traditional folk medication. Clearly, it is not working. He gently prods the child's stomach and back, and is rewarded with a slight grimace. "Kidneys," he says after further prodding. "Probably infected. He needs to get to a hospital."

LaChapelle rises and smiles at the lunacy of the idea. He may as well

Liftoff, Afmadow.

be prescribing Disneyland. "He'll probably die in a couple of days, but I'll leave him some antibiotics," he says without enthusiasm, for he's been told the Somalis will promptly sell any medicine they're given.

"Not much else we can do," the corpsman says heavily.

At midafternoon the Marines collapse their perimeter back to LZ Robin. Their search has turned up one or two old guns. A few Post-it notes flutter in the hot breeze. Chris Bashore, the MEU surgeon, has treated two hundred people at the medical clinic, mostly cases of malnutrition and parasites. Many of his patients need prolonged care. None will get it. "It's hard to leave," says Bashore, looking around at the human misery.

Before they pull out, the Marines empty several dozen jerry cans of

Afmadow.

water out onto the ground. The water wasn't needed, and there's no need to haul it back to the *Wasp*, which makes its own fresh water. To Somalis, fresh, clean water is as precious as life. A couple of Somali children cavort in the puddles. The rest of the crowd watches sullenly as the water gurgles away into the dirt.

A few days later, intelligence reports indicate that caches of weapons that had been stored in Afmadow were indeed moved out the night before the raid, and moved back in after the Marines left. The townspeople are reported to be angry and hostile toward Americans.

"I could go up there again and grab those weapons," Broderick says. "Or I could send helos over the town every night for a week and then move in and take the stuff. I can play with their minds, too."

Clearly, it will take a sustained effort to set the conditions for peace to return to southern Somalia. "I'd like to stick around and kind of get involved," says Broderick.

No luck. The next day he is ordered to pull his men out of the region and move north to Mogadishu. Afmadow and Doobhley will fester on their own.

QUESTION: If there is one single reason why you stay in the Marine Corps and put up with the family separation, what's the reason?

I have met many men, officers and enlisted, that really deserve to be Marines. . . . They know what it takes and are willing to make the necessary sacrifices to make us the world's premiere fighting force. Those guys keep me motivated and make me want to hang around.
—First Lieutenant, Infantry

Just the satisfaction of seeing the mission complete. Somalia will always be fucked up, but I'm proud that I served there, and maybe indirectly my squad helped to save some lives.
—Corporal, Infantry

QUESTION: What single reason would cause you to leave the Marine Corps?

If I died.
—Staff Sergeant, Intelligence

7

HOMETOWN
CAMP LEJEUNE, NORTH CAROLINA
April and May 1993

While the *Wasp* cruises off the sullen Somali coast, George Fenton gets a letter from his wife, Vicky. It is what she calls a "smoker." She is an auburn-haired Georgian of extraordinary good humor and patience. But there are times when those qualities are defeated by the stifling weight of being a military wife and a single parent.

This is one of those times. The lease is expiring on their rented farmhouse outside Camp Lejeune, and she can't find another house. The car needs fixing, their four kids—Kelly, Jessica, Kevin, and Patrick—are a handful, and she broke off part of a tooth. And she's had it with George telling her how wonderful she is for raising the family while he's away. That's shirking his responsibilities a little too glibly.

"That stinks!" she scrawls, and signs the letter not "Love, Vicky" but just "Vicky."

George dispatches back home a letter which Vicky shares with their four children. "You all seem to handle the frustration and hardships with great tolerance," he writes, "and I know I make them worse by being gone. . . . Love to each of you. . . ."

Vicky's outbursts are rare, despite the pain that their life-style imposes on the Fentons and other military families. ("But when we communicate, we *communicate!*" Vicky says.) She has learned to accept the long separations and to deal with the nomadic rootlessness of military life.

"It's kind of what we have been given," she says with a tight smile.

"Over the years, you learn to tolerate things you might not have put up with before," says Vicky, whose ordinarily sunny disposition and casual competence belie a constitution of steel. "We find ways of making it a positive experience."

146

Military service today exacts a heavy toll on tens of thousands of American families, an uncounted price of the new professional military. In past generations, the military services were manned largely by unmarried young volunteers or draftees. Today, 56 percent of the military is married. The Pentagon has under its wing some 2.7 million spouses and children (in the Marine Corps's extended family, wives and children actually outnumber Marines by twenty-four thousand).

Almost two-thirds of the troops who served in the Persian Gulf War left families behind, four times the rate of the Vietnam War.

There are compensations for the separations that characterize today's military life. Unlike many Americans, military families belong to tight-knit communities with strong common values and a sense of moral purpose. Military families tend to make deep friendships. And within relatively small communities like the Marine Corps (there are only 184,000 Marines on active duty), people seem to run into their friends and former neighbors again and again as they move from assignment at one base to another.

Home alone. From left, Vicky Fenton, Jessica, Kevin, Kelly, and neighbor.

Many find it stimulating to uproot themselves and change the scenery every two years or so, and to have the opportunity to live abroad.

"Overall, it has been a positive experience for us," says Vicky Fenton.

Many of today's military professionals work nearly regular hours and get weekends off. Some earn a comfortable living. As a lieutenant colonel, George Fenton pulls down a base pay of over $52,000 a year, plus several hundred dollars a month in untaxed bonuses and allowances. A staff sergeant like Norman North, who is thirty-eight, earns about $32,000 a year in base pay and allowances.

At the lower end of the seniority scale, though, Marine families are just plain poor.

This comes as an unpleasant shock to many new enlistees. Like many Americans, they assumed that the military would take care of all their needs—free child care, medical care, housing, transportation. It does not. A new enlistee fresh out of boot camp often arrives at Camp Lejeune to find that because of his low seniority, he and his wife can't get base housing. They must shell out cash for rent and a security deposit on their apartment. Then they have to buy a car so he can get to work on base, several miles away. Expenses pile up; unscrupulous credit companies move in to loan money at high rates, and soon the young Marine family is deep in debt.

"You can't bring up a family on a Marine's pay," says Lance Corporal Ronnie Gipson, a 24th MEU rifleman whose base salary barely reaches $12,000 a year.

A twenty-two-year-old who enlisted two years ago, Gipson receives $1,001.10 a month in base pay, plus a monthly housing allowance of $329.10. While he is deployed on the *Wasp* for six months, he receives $75.00 a month separation pay, and while the MEU is off the Somali coast, $150 a month "danger pay."

Gipson and his wife Jennifer and their two children (four months and fourteen months old) live in an apartment behind one of Jacksonville's shopping centers. They rented civilian housing when Gipson was assigned to Camp Lejeune and found a twelve-month waiting list for base housing. They pay $385 a month rent and $100 to $200 a month for utilities—close to half of his take-home pay. When he's home and working full time at Camp Lejeune, Gipson bags groceries after hours at the local supermarket to try to make ends met.

Gipson had been stationed at the Kings Bay Navy Base in Georgia when he got hurry-up orders to join the MEU at Camp Lejeune. He spent over $1,000 of their savings to move his family and their belongings, a cost the Marine Corps will reimburse. But six months after the move, Gipson hasn't seen the money. "If you owe them, you gotta pay quick or you get in trouble," he says. "But if they owe you, they take their time."

Gipson's financial predicament is widely typical in the Marine Corps. Roughly half of all Marines are lance corporals or lower in rank, earning even less (a new private receives $9,000 a year basic pay). Brad Myers, a twenty-one-year-old Virginian in the MEU's Weapons Company, was promoted from lance corporal to corporal soon after the *Wasp* sailed for Somalia. That earned him $85.20 a month more in basic pay. Still, he muses one day aboard the *Wasp*, "My little sister earns more money than I do." She's a full-time college student holding down part-time jobs in a computer lab and a toy store.

"That's humiliating," says Myers.

Within the 24th MEU, two-thirds of the Marines under thirty, married with children, reported in a survey that they are "just squeezing by" financially. Six percent said they are "in serious debt."

Among the forty thousand Marines assigned to Camp Lejeune, including the 24th MEU's twenty-one hundred Marines, there are 142 whose families receive food stamps, according to the Onslow County financial assistance office. These are families of at least three people, with a gross monthly income of under $1,289 (many Marines say they would "never" accept food stamps, even if they were qualified). The county also provides Medicaid payments to Marine families to help pay for medicine and dental care not covered by the military health care system.

The Navy–Marine Corps Relief Society, funded by donations and not tax dollars, also provides financial assistance to struggling Marine families. During the twelve months the 24th MEU is in training or deployed in Somalia, the Lejeune chapter gave $131,571 in loans or grants to young Marines who got married during their first term of enlistment and subsequently ran into financial trouble.

"In general, Marines are paid more than many people in the county," says Gen Scott, director of Onslow County's economic services. "But we have a lot of Marine families who don't know how to control their money and they have no extended family in the area."

Financial pressure is not the only stress on military families. An increasing number of them are also bearing the direct cost of today's shrinking military.

Since 1987, the active-duty armed services have experienced a net

149

loss of 553,000 people (the Marine Corps has shrunk by 25,400). But they have lost almost none of their missions. American warships still patrol the Persian Gulf and the northwest Pacific, the Army and Air Force operate out of Korea and Japan, and the Marines are deployed to keep an eye on trouble spots which seem to be growing in number.

That means those who serve work harder, and orders to overseas service seems to come more frequently.

For the Marines of the 24th MEU, this has a hard, immediate impact: When they return from this six-month "float" in August 1993, many of them will begin preparing for another float and will depart in January 1994. In the past, they have been allowed a year or more between six-month floats.

"This is my last enlistment," says thirty-one-year-old Johnny Russ, a sergeant. Russ grew up as an Army brat, bouncing around the country. After ten and a half years in the Marine Corps, he has decided that "it's not worth losing my family over. I don't mean my wife would leave me because I stay in the Corps, but that I'm losing touch with my family. The size of the Corps keeps going down and we're being asked to do more with less," says Russ.

"I spent more time at home when the Cold War was on," he says ruefully.

At any given time in today's peacetime military, some 250,000 servicemen—and increasingly, servicewomen—are serving "unaccompanied" tours of duty overseas, deployed on ships and at remote air bases and on months-long assignments to places like Somalia and Bosnia.

Home alone, the wives struggle with mediocre incomes, chicken pox and homework and cars that won't start. Disciplining children is more difficult with the husband gone. ("Dad would never treat me like this," is a favorite rejoinder of the military child.)

The wives struggle against the institutional anonymity of the military's medical systems and its vast bureaucracies for distributing pay and benefits and housing. Most have seen their own career hopes strangled by frequent moves and by the intense competition among thousands of wives for a handful of low-paying jobs in places like Jacksonville, N.C. They struggle with loneliness and frustration and with con artists who prey on the families of troops deployed overseas.

They receive no medals; they are cheered in no parades. Wives are not memorialized in granite among the heroes' tombstones in America's vast military cemeteries.

Maintaining a cohesive family under these circumstances is difficult. When a unit like the 24th MEU deploys for six months, it drives a wedge deep into the tightest-knit families.

The Marines, thrown together in high-stress conditions, sustain themselves with an intense camaraderie from which their families are forever excluded. The danger and fear and exhilaration of a "real-world" mission like Somalia forges the Marines' camaraderie and accountability into a white-hot love that many Marines say surpasses anything they feel for their wives and families back home.

"We took a bunch of guys who couldn't stand each other and made 'em into a team that would die for each other," says Boatswain's Mate Tony Madden, a pilot for one of the MEU's LCAC Hovercraft. Putting his arm around First Sergeant Michael Cicarrelli, he says, "I know if I'm on the beach and somebody is shooting at us, this guy would put his body in front of the bullets. I love this guy," he says.

Sentiment like that, nourished by shared hardship and by the Marines' own sense of duty and honor and sacrifice, helps explain why they endure and even seek out long months of sea duty.

"It's the right thing to do," says Lieutenant Colonel Preston, the MEU's executive officer. "Twenty-two years ago I took an oath, and it is ingrained in me as deep as anything. My mission is to defend our principles so that my family can go about its business."

The Marines, he says, "are the outer periphery of America."

Preston carries also a deep emotional attachment to his family, particularly to his eldest son, who was born handicapped. The walls of his cramped office aboard the *Wasp* are festooned with drawings by his kids and photos of them and his wife, Linda.

"It's not a great life," Preston acknowledges. "It's hard on the family. It is hard for them to understand.

"But I love it," he concludes.

At home, the wives cope without benefit of the camaraderie and sense of mission that sustains the Marines. It is of little comfort to most wives that their husbands are engaged on an important national mission. "I don't care where he is or whether the country appreciates what he's doing," says one wife. "He's just gone."

Janet Rogers was pregnant when her husband, Lance Corporal Scott Rogers, left with the 24th MEU in February. The baby came in March, when the MEU was deep in the chaos of Somalia. At Camp Lejeune, Janet was alone; like most young military wives, her own parents live far away. The newborn infant, Ashley, stopped breathing and was rushed into intensive care, where she was revived. Janet dealt with the crisis. Scott found out about it later, when there was nothing he could do.

Husbands and wives are shaped and reshaped by such experiences which the other can never really share; each struggles and grows independent in the process. Communication, an inexact art between the closest of civilian couples, is difficult during the Marines' deployment. Marines on the *Wasp* can buy a telephone card enabling them to use the ship's satellite phone. (When it is working, it costs $32 for five minutes.) "Phone card's a macho thing," says Staff Sergeant North. "You buy one and hold on to it. If you call home two weeks after you leave, you're a pooterboy. Guys are going, 'Hell, I can make it to three weeks . . . five weeks!'"

On the rare occasions when the *Wasp* puts into port, the USO will arrange to have dockside phone banks set up, and they are jammed with Marines trying to repair their marriages. But during months at sea there are long gaps between mail call—two weeks or longer.

Mostly, communication fails. "There's no way I can describe to my wife what goes on out here," Sergeant Steve McGowin says one day as the *Wasp* steams off the Somali coast. "And I'm sure I don't really understand what Cathy goes through trying to bring up two teenagers."

Jon Flores, the Hell Bitch mechanic, browses through the ship's store one day looking for a special card to send his wife on their wedding anniversary. He had left Lejeune so quickly in February that they barely had time to say good-bye. The best card he can find is a flowery one that says "To Your Anniversary . . ."

"I just crossed off the 'y' so it said 'our' anniversary and sent it," says Flores. "That's really shitty, man."

In family emergencies, Marines can get leave to go home. But with fewer Marines on duty these days, it's harder to get permission. "I don't think the American people can understand the stress that these kids go through," says Sergeant Major Freddie Tellis, who is responsible for about four hundred of the MEU's enlisted Marines. "I had a kid the other day who found out his grandfather was diagnosed with terminal cancer and his grandmother had a heart attack. Used to be we'd send a kid like that home. No more."

All of these family-related problems culminate in a giant headache for the Marine Corps. Its 209,000 dependents are a major distraction from its mission to provide ready fighting forces for the United States. The vast majority (96 percent) of Marines are unmarried when they enlist. But by

Steve
McGowin.

the end of their first four-year term, over half have gotten married.

Surprisingly, the divorce rate among these young married Marines is low: 4 percent, as compared to 9 percent for comparably aged civilians.

The problem is that more than half of these Marines leave the service after their first term of enlistment (four or six years) is completed. That means the Marine Corps must recruit and train replacements—a costly and time-consuming process that strains its resources.

It was against that background that General Carl Mundy, commandant of the Marine Corps, issued orders on August 5, 1993, to phase out the recruiting of married Marines and to require first-term enlistees to obtain counseling from—but not the permission of—their senior officer before getting married.

The idea seemed only common sense to most enlisted Marines and officers. But not to the politicians and opinion makers of Washington. "Outrageous," said Representative Pat Schroeder, Democrat of Colorado and a member of the House Armed Services Committee. "Ridiculous," steamed a *Chicago Sun-Times* editorial. Mundy's orders were so politically incorrect that the Corps "might have been living on another planet," said the *Washington Post*.

Within hours of the new policy becoming public, Defense Secretary Les Aspin had countermanded it. Although the commandant has the authority to change the Corps's policy on marriage, Aspin publicly chastised Mundy for not clearing it with him beforehand. Recognizing that a marriage problem does exist, Aspin ordered a department-wide review. But the idea of accepting only unmarried volunteers for military service, a Pentagon official said, was "dead on arrival."

So the Marines cope.

Aboard the *Wasp*, the senior NCOs and troop commanders have their hands full dealing not just with Somalia, but with problems back home. Captain Harry Bass, who commands the MEU's artillery unit, Sierra Battery, is notified that the wife of one of his Marines has had a miscarriage back at Camp Lejeune. Bass arranges for the Marine to call home, for Lejeune's Family Service Center to see what help the wife needs, and for the Marine to be assigned to work on the flight deck where he receives extra pay.

Charlie Company commander Mark Toal is trying to arrange for one of his Marines to catch up with the *Wasp*. The Marine had been left behind when the MEU sailed in February because his nineteen-year-old wife couldn't cope with a year-old toddler and an ill infant. "Families are my responsibility," says Toal. "When you are leading Marines, their problems are your problems."

(Toal himself is having problems: the Marine Corps has been slightly overpaying his housing allowance for months and Toal now owes the Marine Corps paymaster $2,800. The money has been spent on rent and car payments, but if Toal doesn't pay it immediately, the Marine Corps will withhold his paychecks. Problem is, his wife Jackie has the checkbook, and mail takes weeks. "I could work it out easily if I was at home," he says with frustration.)

George Fenton sits in his stateroom aboard the *Wasp*, struggling over a letter home. His eldest daughter, Kelly, plays a school saxophone in the high school band; she wants her own sax. It would be terrific if he managed to bring one home to her, he thinks. Maybe he could pick one up if the *Wasp* stops for a port call on the way home this summer.

Managing his family relationships, he finds, is much harder than being the operations officer for the MEU. Fenton is like a lot of Marines: He loves his family, and he loves the Marine Corps, and he finds it exceedingly difficult to accommodate them both.

"I miss my family terribly," he says. "My own father was in three wars. We in the family paid the price. We did not have the unity, the richness of family life, because he was gone so much. None of my brothers or sisters wanted that for a life."

Yet George did. From his earliest years, he has dedicated his life to the Marine Corps. When his father was home between combat tours in Korea and Vietnam, he would take young George around to the Marine chow halls. "I thought all that stuff was the neatest thing," George says with a smile. "That's sick, huh?"

In a more serious vein, he acknowledges that his career "is hard on Vicky and the kids. I make the least amount of money of all my siblings. And obviously I'm away a lot. The thing about Marines is, I miss being with them. When you're not here, you miss the closeness. It permeates you, it becomes part of your soul."

He and Vicky met while she was a flight attendant and he was fresh out of the U.S. Military Academy at West Point, N.Y. (In his class of 1974, three graduating cadets chose to be commissioned in the Marine Corps rather than in the Army.) Vicky thought the new Marine lieutenant with an eighth-inch "high and tight" Marine Corps haircut was a little odd. "When I first met him I felt really sorry for him—he had no hair," Vicky recalls with a laugh. His first assignment was to the Marine Corps base on Okinawa. Normally, Okinawa is an "unaccompanied" tour, meaning wives are not authorized. Vicky went anyway and set up house in an apartment outside the base gates.

Over the years, Vicky followed as George won promotions and new assignments. In sixteen years they moved household and children eleven times, bouncing from North Carolina to California to Virginia to California to North Carolina. For George, who was born into a Marine Corps family at the Marine Corps Base at Quantico, Va, this was normal. Not for Vicky, who had grown up in a thoroughly civilian family in the Atlanta suburbs.

"A lot of the [military] housing was shabby and bug-infested, pretty substandard," she says. "And on military bases, you're kind of isolated. It's like going into a big tomb. The ladies would occasionally have Tupperware parties, that kind of thing. And I didn't understand the discrimination, where if you are an officer's wife you wouldn't want to be seen talking to an enlisted wife."

When the Fenton family got orders to Quantico a few years ago, Vicky insisted that they would live like a normal family. She bought them a split-level in the suburbs.

"I was scared to death at the idea of living outside a military base," says George. "But I discovered that I actually liked it. I had neighbors who were professors, orthodontists, all kinds of neat things." Then came orders to Camp Lejeune again. George could move down there by himself and commute the four hours home on weekends, or he could haul the whole family down there. "We held a family meeting and decided to stay together, all move to Lejeune," he says.

"I had hard feelings about it," Vicky says. She had just managed to get a job. "Moving again meant I had to tear the kids out of school and away from their friends, and I had to give up any chance I had of doing a job I really wanted to do," she says. "I told George that we'd never see him anyway, so why should we have to follow him down there? He said, yeah, you'll see me all the time. But we got down here, and he was working twenty hours a day and now he's gone off for six months."

But she coped. The kids came home from their first day at school complaining that the school didn't have a swim team. Okay, said Vicky, "We'll just squirt each other with hoses."

That kind of gritty, make-the-best-of-it determination is much at evidence one day in May as the wives of the 24th MEU gather at a Camp Lejeune picnic grounds for a Family Day. They set out plates of brownies and potato chips and jugs of Kool-Aid. They share gossip, sternly discipline rowdy kids, comfort toddlers, and set up a video camera to tape messages for their absent husbands, gone now for three months.

This Sunday Family Day has the air of a reunion of the survivors of some dimly remembered disaster. Here are women of wildly diverse backgrounds—hardcore conservatives and liberals, Southern Baptists and big-city Jews, farm women and Ivy League elites—thrown together in common bereavement.

"This is one good thing about the separation—I'm making more friends, good close friends, than I do when Will is home," says Jeanne Hartzell, a twenty-nine-year-old from Rutland, Vt. "We're all far away from our families, and our husbands are gone," says Jeanne, whose husband is a watch officer on Broderick's staff. "You have to make your own friends."

Lori Roupp is here, with two-year-old Amanda on her hip. Lori is married to Chris, the sergeant who scurried to get cold soda to the crew of the Hell Bitch and other Marines at Purple Beach in Somalia. She knows nothing of Chris's life on the *Wasp* (she has never seen enlisted berthing) and knows little of what his job involves. She sums up her life this way: "We get to have two kids' birthdays, our anniversary, and Mother's Day, all with Daddy gone."

High-quality day care would help, and the Marine Corps and the other services have tried to provide it. Nationwide, the Marine Corps has built day-care facilities for 10,240 children, but more than 17,000 are turned away each year for lack of space.

Jobs would also help relieve the monotony of being a single-parent homemaker, but jobs are hard to come by around military bases. When George and Vicky Fenton returned from Okinawa to the Marine Corps base at Camp Pendleton, Calif., an optimistic Vicky went job hunting. "I had always worked before we were married," she says. "This time I interviewed and was turned down four times, because I was married to a Marine. They knew I could be gone any day."

Around Camp Lejeune, "All the jobs pay five dollars an hour, whether you're at McDonald's or a nurse or teacher," says Debbie North, Staff Sergeant North's young wife. "They know you're only temporary and they can replace you in a second. They really take advantage of you."

Most Marine wives who work outside the home earn less than five thousand dollars a year before taxes, according to a Defense Department survey released in late 1993.

In desperation, many wives seek graduate degrees, hoping somehow to make a career of their own. Karla Henry, the wife of one of Broderick's logistics officers, commutes three hours a day to work on a master's degree in social work at East Carolina University in Greenville. It is not clear how she will establish a career while bouncing around the country with her husband, Sam, a Marine captain.

"What chance do wives have of a career? Absolutely none!" Debbie North says with indignation.

But unemployment and thwarted careers aren't always the worst problems.

Dena Askew gave up a job as a Russian linguist in the Army to marry

Corporal Matt Askew, who is an Arab translator for the 24th MEU. Now she's at home while he has an intense and exciting career away.

"You get kind of scared that you might grow apart even if you have a strong marriage," says Dena. "We've gone back and forth about this, the benefits of staying in and the difficulty of being apart. It's not fair for me to tell him what to do, but it's not fair to me to keep quiet, either," she says, adding: "I've rehearsed this speech a lot."

"I have bad days too," says Melinda Blaske consolingly. A delicate blonde, she says, "I sit down and do a five-page letter, both sides, and I'm sobbing. Marine Corps marriages," she adds with a sigh, "you just don't know what you're getting into. It's just like, whatever it is, we'll get through it."

"I am trying to be the pillar of steel that this family needs, that Norm needs," says Debbie North, cuddling her fourteen-month-old daughter, Brianna. "Norman called this morning and we talked for a long time, and he said, 'It sounds like you're doing okay with this,' and I said, 'No, I'm not, but *one* of us has to cope.'"

Heidi Poupard is coping and would do it again. Like most Marine wives, she simply fell in love and followed her man Tim into the Corps. Since that time, almost four years ago, Tim has been able to live at home with Heidi and three-year-old Mark for little over a year.

She has recently gotten a letter from Tim saying that he will be home in August as scheduled, but will be thrown almost immediately into intensive training for the next "float" and will be gone from January 1994 through June.

"There are days when my son screams, 'I want my Daddy!'" says Heidi. "But I'm proud of what Tim does. It makes me feel good, knowing that he is doing something important."

These Family Day activities draw only about a third of the MEU's families, says Nina McBroom, whose husband Joel has just managed to get a call through from the *Wasp* only to find no one home. ("He just left a sad message on the answering machine," says Nina.) An experienced federal building manager, she has been unable to find a job here and is volunteering at the Lejeune Family Services Center, helping young families. "This is how I keep my sanity," she.says.

"A lot of the wives don't have a clue about how to get along by themselves," says Nina. "Most of us are a long-distance call away from home, and even if you call they don't really understand what you're going through. A lot of wives are just dumped here, the husbands get transferred in and leave on deployment. The wives are locked in a trailer someplace with kids twenty-four hours a day, and they don't know where to go to get help."

Some apparently help themselves. Out on the *Wasp* one day, the MEU gets a call from the legal office at Camp Lejeune. The young wife of one of their Marines has filed for divorce, has cleaned out their joint bank account, and has gotten a court order to get part of his paychecks for child support. Thanks to infrequent mail deliveries to the *Wasp* off the Somali coast, the jilted Marine is unware of all this, and has been bouncing checks—an unforgivable sin in the Marine Corps code of conduct.

In another instance, a Marine's wife cleans out their bank account, climbs in the new car he bought just before the MEU left in February, and takes off, never to be seen again. The Marine finds out about this when he is advised that his car payments are months overdue.

Gossip and anecdotal evidence suggests that some Marine wives find solace in the arms of other Marines—just as their husbands may be tempted to stray during boisterous liberty in foreign ports.

"There is infidelity on both sides," says Jeanne Hartzell. "It's extremely easy here—the town is full of bars and the bars are packed."

Far less visible in the stoic bonhomie of military life are alcoholism and child abuse. For years, these problems have silently ravaged families under the stress of military life. And military custom has dictated that such family problems be kept strictly within the family, for fear of jeopardizing the husband's career.

Retired Army general H. Norman Schwarzkopf, who led allied forces in the Persian Gulf War, grew up in an Army family. He recalls that his alcoholic mother, who drank heavily during his father's extended absences, made life miserable for him. Yet for years she hid her drinking from her husband and his fellow officers. "It was something you didn't talk about," Schwarzkopf later recalled. Besides, he added, "the Army was a hard-drinking world."

Heavy drinking in the military ranks has decreased significantly since 1980, according to the results of an extensive study sponsored by the Defense Department and published in 1993. However, the study examined only active-duty military personnel; the drinking habits of military spouses and families were ignored. According to the author of the study, Dr. Robert M. Bray, of the Research Triangle Institute in North Carolina, there has been no systematic study of alcoholism or drug abuse among military dependents.

Child and spouse abuse is slightly more visible. In fiscal 1992, the most recent year for which statistics are available, the military services recorded fourteen cases of child abuse per one thousand population, a rate significantly lower than the twenty-five cases per one thousand reported for the civilian population.

In a growing recognition of the problem, the Pentagon in 1993 spent $62 million to deal with child and spouse abuse, three times what it spent in 1991. Altogether, the Defense Department spends $2.4 billion a year on family-related programs.

Amid all these problems, life goes on. At the subdued festivities of the 24th MEU's Family Day, Anna Roberts suddenly goes into labor and is rushed off to the hospital with her five-year-old daughter, Kristie, in tow. Husband Eddie, an artillery coordinator, will miss the birth and the first difficult and joyful months of his second child's life.

George Fenton's youngest son, nine-year-old Patrick, is already yearning to be a Marine. Of the four Fenton children, he is the one who

Anna Roberts and daughter Kristie.

looks most like his dad, right down to the freckles and impish grin. He is short, too, and a scrapper in sports. In games around the house, he organizes his brother and sisters into teams and issues brusque orders as they haul a GI Joe in an empty soda can on a string up and down from a balcony. Patrick misses his Dad and proudly wears a United States Marine Corps T-shirt.

On the other side of the world, the USS *Wasp* receives a visit from General Colin Powell. Five months away from retirement, the chairman of the Joint Chiefs of Staff tells Marines and sailors assembled on the flight deck that together, they make up a real family.

They are, Powell tells them, "a family not bound together by blood relations, but an even closer family bound together by sacrifice, shared commitment, by being professionals in that proud group of Americans willing to serve their country. . . .

"I am enormously proud," says Powell. "You carry the values of the nation from generation to generation."

The Corps is a lot smaller than any other services, but we are the first ones to see combat and [are] on the front lines the majority of the time. We are deployed away a lot more than any other service. We are away from our families more than we are with them and some of the time, like me, we lose our family due to the service.
—Sergeant, Helicopter Mechanic

Since I have been in the Marine Corps we have always fallen short. It seems as though we are in the lower class bracket instead of being middle class. I go to different countries and place my life in God's care, not really knowing if a sniper will shoot me this time or next, while a person can play a sport or sit behind a desk and have only one worry—what to eat for lunch.
—Sergeant, Infantry

In order to have a real family with love and togetherness, the Marines are out. I've been married eight of the past ten years in service. I've seen my family approximately three and a half out of eight because of floats, war, and training. I need out 'cause I want to be a husband, not a fling once in a while, and a father, not some stranger who stops in for a few months. . . . Sorry, but that's the facts.
—Sergeant, Infantry

8

LOCK 'N' LOAD
MOGADISHU, SOMALIA

April 1993

Charlie Company's 1st Platoon moves out at 1600 hours, following warily behind Corporal Richard Diaz. He is from Las Vegas. He is twenty-one years old.

Diaz unhooks a section of concertina razor wire, jams a magazine into his rifle and chambers a round. Behind him, eleven "ratchet-clicks" indicate the rest of the patrol is locked and loaded as the Marines slip out of their compound into the late-afternoon sun.

Behind them is home, Checkpoint 77: a bombed-out, burned-out six-story hulk that once housed Mogadishu's main bank. It is flanked with sandbagged guard posts and armed guards. Neatly lettered across the blackened main doorway is this legend: UNITED STATES MARINE CORPS SEMPER FIDELIS.

High on the top floor, Charlie Company has sandbagged the window holes, stacked cases of MREs and bottled water, and set up mildewed cots on the grimy, blackened cement floor. Marines have also rigged an ingenuous piss tube. Constructed of empty water bottles fitted together into a long pipe, it stretches from the gutted bathroom on the sixth floor down to a cistern in the basement, with intake funnels on each floor.

In front of 1st Platoon is a square mile of rubble, dust, and fetid squalor, all that is left of what was once Mogadishu's posh diplomatic quarter. For two years, competing Somali militias armed with the superpowers' most lethal infantry weapons have swept back and forth over this small piece of ground with no apparent result except its utter destruction.

The Marines of 1st Platoon are in charge here. Most are twenty or twenty-one, smart American kids, well trained as military professionals. In this neighborhood, they are mayor, city council, beat cops, trauma medics, and SWAT team. They are responsible for taking the policy made in Washington and making it work here.

Diaz is an old hand in this neighborhood. He was among the first Marines that President Bush ordered to Somalia in December 1992. Bush has retired to Houston. Richard Diaz is still here. His desert utilities are bleached almost white by the relentless sun.

Diaz is a handsome, wiry youth. Back home, he would be indistinguishable in a crowd of jiving, wisecracking kids in a McDonald's parking lot.

Here, Diaz is a master. He holds his weapon carefully and steps with measured gait up the street. There is no talking. He directs the platoon with hand signals: Spread out. Hold up. Move. Freeze. In the rubble of what once were embassies and mansions, in the shadows of stinking alleyways where raw sewage bakes in the sun, a dozen snipers could be lurking. Gunfire aimed at Marines here is common. Eight Americans have been killed since December, fifteen wounded. The toll will go higher.

Diaz is confident and careful. It is eerily quiet. The swirling crowds of taunting street urchins are gone; only an occasional pedestrian flits down a side street. Warily, the Marines step around rusted shell casings and a furry carcass rotting in the dirt. Broken glass crunches underfoot. Sweat soaks through fatigues and then through heavy flak jackets. When Diaz motions his men across an intersection, sparkling droplets of sweat flick off his hand.

Eighteen minutes into the patrol, a shot snaps through the air.

Instantly Diaz darts into a dark doorway in pursuit of the sniper. Behind him, 1st Platoon Marines drop to their knees, leaning against the rubbled walls, heads swiveling, eyes alert, pulses pounding. A woman standing in the alley freezes, her hand to her mouth. Chris McDonald sprints bent over to the doorway where Diaz has disappeared. Rifle up, he stands panting against the wall, ready to crash through the doorway if there is trouble. ("I wasn't afraid, just a little nervous," McDonald says later. "Shit, I grew up in L.A. I'm used to this." But the wad of tobacco he had clenched behind his lower lip left an indentation that lasted for hours.)

After a minute or two, Diaz emerges. He pushes his helmet up and wipes his forhead. Then he silently motions the patrol on down the street. The sniper has gotten away. He will be back.

View from Checkpoint 77.

Combat patrol, Mogadishu.

Charlie Company arrives in Mogadishu.

First Platoon came ashore early this morning, along with the rest of Charlie Company. They had staged at zero-dark thirty on the *Wasp*'s hangar deck, waited an hour, then trooped down the ramp onto the LCACs and into a diabolical device called a "Makesh." That's how the Marine Corps pronounces *MCESHS*, for Marine Corps Expeditionary Shelter System. It is a large, windowless box lashed to the deck of the LCAC. The Marines crammed inside and sat down in the black heat

and prayed for calm seas. ("You don't wanna be in here when somebody gets seasick," says a Marine. "You ever heard of the word *epidemic*?")

On the beach, Charlie Company meets Ed Lesnowicz. He is a lieutenant colonel, commanding the battalion of Marines that got to Mogadishu in December. The 24th MEU's Charlie Company will be working with his men for a week, familiarizing themselves with the city and the business of peacekeeping.

Lesnowicz is a short, swarthy man with a cigar and an attitude. The attitude is a fierce devotion to his men's welfare. He has lost a man to sniper fire. He does not intend for it to happen again.

He fires up his cigar and motions for Charlie Company to gather around. It is eight A.M., and the sky and sand and sea have blended into a seamless steel-colored burning irritation. Mark Toal, Charlie Company's commander, has authorized his men to wear their soft desert hats and carry their helmets on their belts. That will change.

Toal and Lesnowicz confer.

Cathedral, Mogadishu.

"We control this town," Lesnowicz growls. "This is a military operation run by a company of infantrymen and clerks and cooks, using what they were taught in boot camp. If you're a United States Marine, you can do anything."

"Roger that, sir," says Toal.

"The first coupla days we'll start out slow, ninety miles an hour," says Lesnowicz. "We work like whirling dervishes. How many men ya got?"

"Hundred sixty-five," says Toal.

"Let's do it," says Lesnowicz.

Mogadishu checkpoint.

Toal (left), staff officers.

"This is not a safe place," he bellows in his welcoming speech to Charlie Company. "You're here to do a peaceful mission in an unpeaceful place. It's not an easy mission. It's not in any books. Luck counts."

He spits, replaces the cigar stub in his mouth, and puffs reflectively. Charlie Company, squatting in the sand in a circle around Lesnowicz, waits in awed silence.

"You'll be working with my men, six hours on checkpoint, six hours on patrol. You get six hours to sleep, eat, and write letters home. Then you're back on patrol."

Spit. Puff.

"It is likely you will be shot at on a daily basis. I don't wanna send anybody else home, so keep your heads screwed on. Helmets and flaks are essential, always. Good luck."

"Welcome to hell," mutters Steve Conway.

Charlie Company spreads out to bivouac around the city, riding in trucks that attract almost every kid in the city. There is something universal about the children who attend American military operations. In Philip Caputo's classic account of Vietnam, *A Rumor of War*, he describes how kids would run along behind Marines' convoys, yelling things like "GI gimme one cig'rette, hey gimme candy hey booshit, fuck you GI numbah ten!" Here, the kids are yelling: "Hey! Mah-reen numbah one. Haaaay, Ah-mereeka! Gimme cig'rette!"

But their understanding of English is limited. One boy, perhaps twelve years old, waves at the Marines happily. "Get the fuck outta here, bitch!" he shouts in greeting.

Toal commandeers a Humvee and takes a tour, noting local ambush spots and checking in to see that his men are settling down okay. Marines are everywhere in evidence, manning checkpoints, patrolling along dusty streets and through the city's gutted Italian-built cathedral and inside the teeming central marketplace, where women tend tables of watermelons and oranges and flyblown meat carcasses. Toal watches Somali men hammering and painting new market stalls.

"City's coming back," he notes approvingly.

At one barbed-wire checkpoint near a collapsed two-story concrete building, a crowd of young Somali toughs confronts a black Marine with a mixture of awed curiosity and derision as the Marine, his rifle slung, works to pick up some useful new Somali phrases.

Toal climbs to the roof of the gutted former national police headquarters building, high on a windy hilltop. The tortured city spreads out beneath him. Someone points out the distant ruins of the cathedral, where looters stole from the crypt the body of the Italian bishop who founded the cathedral generations ago.

"We'd better get to know this place," says Toal. "I have a feeling we're going to be back."

Eddie Adams is getting to know the place. He is seeing the misery and squalor of Mogadishu in biblical terms. "Why does God allow this to go on?" he wonders one afternoon as he cleans his weapon high in the burned-out bank building. "My heart goes out to the Somalis. I pray for them. I touched the children, I was crying, 'Why? Why?'

"Well, they are all Muslims," says Adams. "And God said, thou shalt worship no other god but me. They are worshipping the wrong god. The

Eddie Adams, Checkpoint 77.

Lord has taught me what happens when you reject Him. I know this is the word of God. Spiritually, this experience has taught me a lot. I am still grieving for them."

Nick Smith also is getting to know the place. He and his three-man fire team were dropped off at an observation post on the second floor of an abandoned building near the marketplace. They were assigned to share rotating patrols with some of Lesnowicz's men. The long day dragged on. At one point, shots were fired. Smith and his men dashed out to the street; the snipers had vanished. The Marines stalked through the jostling, sullen crowds. That solemn twelve-year-old girl might be holding a hand grenade behind her back. That doorway deep in shadow might be hiding a sniper. The heat and noise and dust were relentless.

Smith and his men were supposed to be relieved at dusk. Dusk arrived but the relief didn't. Soon it was evident that they were marooned in this hostile city, miles from the relative safety of their bivouac at Checkpoint 77, the burned-out bank building. Smith realized it was up to him ("You are responsible for the lives of your buddies"). He is a lance corporal, twenty-one years old.

According to the book, Nick Smith had not been the model Marine. Eighteen months ago on guard duty back at Camp Lejeune, on a bitter cold night, he tried to warm himself by lighting kerosene in an empty soda can. He was caught and sentenced to additional guard duty. But he didn't serve it: He paid another Marine to stand duty in his place. He was caught again, docked a week's pay, and sentenced to a week in the Correction Control Unit, a boot camp for wayward Marines.

Now, Smith took a deep breath and led his men out on the street. He had no radio, no map, no compass. He thought he could find his way back home. He formed the men up by the book: point, flanks, rear. It was dark, the most dangerous time in the city. There was no electricity; the only light came from a half moon and occasional explosions in the distance.

"If we got ambushed, it was pretty much over," he said later. "It crossed our minds."

After hours of walking, Smith got his fire team home. Later he was awarded the Navy Achievement Medal.

That kind of responsibility and accountability get heavier in the higher ranks. Harry Bass muses about this late one night in Mogadishu. Bass commands the MEU's artillery unit, Sierra Battery, of 123 Marines.

He is twenty-nine and has rapidly thinning blond hair and a goofy grin. Artillery is a precise science and art. Bass says three of the Marine Corps's twelve battery commanders have been relieved of command in the past six months because they were imprecise. He takes command so seriously that the other company commanders kid him about it.

Bass can take it. He grew up dirt-poor in Meridian, Miss., in a viciously self-destructive family. He worked his way out, excelling in Boy Scouts and academics. Bass was not a college athletic star like many Marine officers. He is more of a thinker, and he has thought deeply about Somalia.

"Sometimes you have to cool down Marines," he says. "They get fired up and forget their own mortality. You gotta go to them and say, 'You realize this is for real? This is not TV.'

"A certain amount of fear is healthy. In Sierra Battery we teach kids to put ordnance on time, on target. But who's the target? You are not trained to consider that these are real people. We don't consider that. We tell kids in boot camp we're training them to be killers. Just doing a job. Do they really understand what that means, to put rounds on an enemy position? No—especially if the target's twenty klicks [kilometers] away."

Bass pauses in the soft night air. In the distance, shots echo over the city and a helo clatters invisibly across the sky.

"Until Somalia, I'd never seen a dead body," Bass says. "I felt distanced from it; it wasn't from anything I had done. It's such an alien culture out there. You get Marines worked up, you peak 'em, but still you gotta tell 'em, this is for real. If they think too much about killing, that's a mistake. On the other hand, you have to make your Marines understand that Somalis are human and real. All the aggressiveness needs a sanity check. You may be killing somebody else. You may get killed yourself. This is not TV.

"I've got eighteen- and nineteen-year-olds out there with authority in five-man squads. I don't seek to throw my Marines into a situation like this. They're out there on the streets in the crowds. I had a Marine get knifed the other day.

"But I've never seen my battery tighter than they are now," Bass says with satisfaction. "They all want to be here and to make a difference, and they all feel they are making a difference."

It is hard to tell whether the men of Charlie Company's 1st Platoon feel they are making a difference.

Mogadishu patrol.

They are plodding along with their dripping helmets casting long shadows over their faces, two single files on each side of the street, each man a careful twenty paces from the next. They pass a woman sitting on a broken chair outside a darkened doorway. Inexplicably, she is crooning "Old MacDonald Had a Farm" to the baby on her lap. "Eeeeyi, eeeeyi oh," follows the Marines down the street. At an intersection Diaz holds up his hand and the patrol pauses. He peers around the corner, then quickly crosses into a lane and motions. The men cross one by one, each covered by the others.

A pickup truck careens around the corner a block away and accelerates toward the patrol. A dozen Somalis perch precariously on it, waving rifles and hooting and cheering. The truck flies a banner proclaiming "Feed the Children," one of the private agencies working in Mogadishu. Diaz waves politely as the truck and its passengers rocket past. The men are "guards" for the agency, he says, so they are allowed to have weapons. After a minute or two he adds, "It's not a policy everybody agrees with."

On down the dusty lane. A child has neatly arranged dried feces, human or dog, in a pattern in the dirt. The Marines step across a puddle clogged with half a grapefruit rind and a dead rooster. Dust is caking on their sweaty faces and hands. Their clothes reek with Mogadishu's sour smell of smoke and urine. They pass a once-elegant villa whose roof has collapsed. Rubble spills out the windows, but scarlet bougainvillea flourishes on the wall surrounding what might once have been a lawn. The wall is pockmarked with the peculiar signature of heavy-caliber weapons: a deep hole the size of a fist, with finger-deep shrapnel marks in the cement radiating out from the center like a child's drawing of the sun.

Back in Washington, Operation Restore Hope, the U.S.-led intervention in Somalia, has been declared a major success. Under pressure from Congress, U.S. forces are being called home.

This word hasn't reached Diaz and 1st Platoon. The setting sun bathes them in a rosy glow as they turn homeward toward Checkpoint 77. There, a new patrol is suiting up, pulling on their gritty, sweat-soaked utilities, shrugging on damp flak jackets, snapping their helmet chin straps and checking canteens and ammo and first aid kits. In a few hours, 1st Platoon itself will be back on patrol, and again, and again. It seems never to end—the heat, the stench, the exhaustion, the danger.

A solitary man walks toward them. Diaz motions to him to raise his shirt. The man does so. He is not hiding a weapon. He probably is not the sniper who shot at the patrol a few minutes ago. Diaz waves him off, and the man walks away, eyes averted.

Diaz turns, covering the man with his rifle, watching him safely out of sight. Then Diaz turns and motions the men forward. The patrol plods on into the fading light.

QUESTION: Has your experience in the Marine Corps generally been better than you expected when you joined, about the same, or not as good? Why?

Not as good. A hurry-up-and-wait outfit and someone else always gets credit for what you do or your unit does.
—Corporal, Machine Gunner

Better. You stand out from others and have a certain pride no other [service] has.
    —Corporal, Amphibious Assault Vehicles

No, it is not what I expected. But it hasn't hurt me, either. It opened my eyes to the world and gave me some money to play with. Hell, I'm twenty-one years old and been around the world twice.
    —Corporal, Amphibious Assault Vehicles

We are a tight group of men regardless of games or bullshit. We all know our job and we're honest and I trust Marines with my life and they trust me with theirs. That's something civilians don't understand. We have a hard job some-times and we are the best at what we do and I'm proud of any Marine regardless of if he's a shitbird because I know what he had to do to get here.
    —Private 1st Class, Infantry

9

JERK-EX
SOMALIA
April/June 1993

On a panel torn from a cardboard carton of MREs, Captain Tim Hederer keeps a journal of the days in April that Bravo Company, which he commands, spends in an upcountry Somali town called Goob Weyn. It is a chronicle of frustration.

"No open hostilities," Hederer carefully prints at the end of their first day of patrolling and manning checkpoints. "Will con't patrolling in AM . . . confisc. variety of knives and swords, 7.62 machine gun and 2-300 heavy machine gun ammo." Technically, that is enough to wipe out Hederer's entire company.

Bandits, the temporarily idle soldiers of the warlords, are harassing this region of gently rolling farmland along the Juba River in southern Somalia. The UN has stationed Belgian troops nearby, but there are too few of them. Stick-thin market women are ambushed and robbed of their produce. Weapons are seeping out of the warlords' caches in places like Doobhley and Afmadow and are being gathered in clan strongholds. Bodies dumped along the roadside indicate that revenge killings are increasing.

April 11, Easter Sunday. "Build-up of Somali males in town," Hederer records. "Men & women come in from north but only women leave, usu. at night. Somali road block between A and B [companies] continues to be a problem. Have not yet been able to locate and apprehend individuals involved. Cache [weapons] hunt continues to turn up negative."

While Bravo Company struggles to apply Washington's policy to Goob Weyn, Broderick's other Marines are busy elsewhere. They are aggressively patrolling the streets of Mogadishu and Kismayu. They deliver grain to outlying villages, set up one-day medical and dental clinics in which they treat some 1,500 Somalis. In the village of Baar, whose crops are periodically wiped out by floods, the Marines bring in their bulldozer and build a nine-foot-high, 168-foot-long levee. The work takes four eighteen-hour days. The villagers respond by inviting the Marines to a soiree of singing and drumming and dancing.

These humanitarian operations are fun, constructive, and "feel good," says Kevin Humphrey, a twenty-year-old lance corporal from Joplin, Mo. But they don't seem to be aimed at any grand strategic goal.

There's no war being won here, and definitely no sign of the political reconciliation and social and economic progress that the United Nations was supposed to bring. For every village of Baar with a new levee, there are hundreds of villages where the majority have died from starvation or war, or have fled to the cities to be swept up in the brutal civil conflict.

Many Marines feel they could be put to better use. They are, after all, the best warriors of the most powerful nation on earth. The warlords and their skinny fighters are no match for Marines. But this is a peacekeeping mission, not war. The Marines storm into a town like Afmadow, then leave. They're dropped into Goob Weyn, then leave. Unseen higher authorities, politicians, jerk them here and there, seemingly without purpose.

"Jerk-ex," pronounces Staff Sergeant North.

If Broderick has misgivings about his mission in Somalia, he rarely voices them. He has his orders. ("See what you can do. Don't become decisively engaged.") Within the limits of his authority, he is trying to keep his men productively active and to achieve temporary—if not lasting—results in the parts of Somalia in which he is allowed to operate.

"Frustrating as hell," he admits.

Hederer has the same problem. He is a handsome, sandy-haired thirty-year-old from Marshfield, Wis. Like his colleague Mark Toal, who commands Charlie Company, Hederer knows this is his one shot at commanding a company in a "real world" situation. This is not some exercise. His fellow captains would kill for this opportunity. Hell, so would most Marine generals. (As officers rise through the ranks, they become increasingly distanced from the grunts they love. "Being a company commander was the best job I ever had," says a wistful Brigadier General Paul K. Van

Riper, commanding general of the 24th MEU's parent unit, the 2nd Marine Division.)

Goob Weyn is billed as a two-day operation. It goes twenty. The men of Bravo, who had brought along two days' worth of socks and smokes, consider this a typical betrayal by higher authorities. Hederer, though, is in his element. There is no government here, no police force, no laws. Hederer and his men are it. Even Broderick is far way, back on the *Wasp* off the coast. Hederer is excited about the possibilities here. We're Americans. We can fix it.

He holds long talks each day with the elders of the town, listening to their gossip and ideas and complaints. Through an interpreter, he learns that they are worried about the warlords, angry at the bandits, and concerned about some of their own people being detained by Belgian troops. Hederer passes these up the chain of command and does what he can to mediate between the townspeople and the layers of U.S. and UN bureaucracy above him.

For the first few nights Bravo is bivouacked outside Goob Weyn, Somali families camp beside them, apparently glad of the protection. But after a few days they begin to drift away, and boredom overtakes the men of Bravo. Friction develops over small issues. The enlisted men complain about having to constantly wear their heavy helmets and flak jackets (Belgians wear jaunty red berets and, occasionally, shorts).

"Sitting out there on roadblock day after day, night after night was boring and kind of scary," one of Hederer's Marines says later. "You'd see flares going off and you don't know who was who or what was going on.

"We played chess on an MRE case using snuff cans and Tabasco bottles and a .50-cal round. One day this kid comes up, he must've been around nine, and he points to the round and says, 'Browning fifty.' When I was that age I sure didn't know what a Browning fifty [caliber machine gun] was. These Somali kids, they're somethin' else."

April 13. "Combined Bravo and Charlie Co. raid on eastern side of river comes up empty," Hederer writes. "One rifle lost in river [the Marine rifle was recovered by divers the next day] . . . one dead Somali found at river crossing. Animal attack seems to be the cause."

"It was stupid, a waste of time," says an enlisted Marine. "After a while our attitude was, 'Fuck it.' We never found any weapons. We'd have women and children at the checkpoint, and we could see other people going way out around us a couple of klicks [kilometers] away. That's where the weapons were going, but we didn't have permission to go out there.

"We had this one guy, he'd come around every day just to practice his English. Said he used to have a good job but everything was destroyed during the war, and he's got nothing to do but to be a fighter now."

The Marine pauses to light a cigarette. "He'd come around chow time. We'd talk for hours. One day he says, you know, as soon as you guys leave things'll go back the way they were. To war. All you're doing is prolonging it. Which I kinda understood his point."

Two days later, Hederer records: "Raid was planned on Somalis conducting possible weapons smuggling the night before. No strange activity seen so raid [was] aborted."

After almost three weeks, Bravo is withdrawn back to the ship. "I think we kept weapons from moving through there while we were there," Hederer says. "At one time I had 320 people, but even that wasn't enough to do what I wanted to do. We should have done more weapons sweeps, more medical clinics. We should have gotten out more to the small outlying villages to see what we could do to help. But with what we had, I'm not sure what more our company could have done."

One of Hederer's corpsmen agrees that more medical clinics might have helped. "But we didn't have enough supplies to do that," he says. "We just had what we needed to take care of our own."

As Bravo is getting back aboard ship for its first hot showers in three weeks, the Hell Bitch and her crew are being put ashore in another convoy, this time to haul forty-two tons of grain from Kismayu up along the Juba River for distribution by civilian relief agencies. The operation goes uneventfully, but on the way back the Hell Bitch's radio crackles into life. "Doc, we got a problem!"

Up ahead, the convoy's lead vehicle has been flagged down by a Somali boy. His brother is bleeding and needs help. A corpsman is promised, and the call goes back to Daryl Kyllonen on the Hell Bitch. As the vehicle bounces toward the head of the column, Kyllonen frets. "All they told me is a guy's bleeding and I didn't know where or why," Kyllonen recalled later. "Usually I can get my anxiety over and get my plan ready, but there was nothing I could do until I got there."

It is the worst possible news. A teenager had been playing with a rocket-propelled grenade ("Probably getting ready to throw it at us," says Staff Sergeant North). It exploded, the sharpnel ripping into his chest and tearing open a lung. "Oh, shit," Kyllonen murmurs as he kneels down and opens his bag. A crowd of about fifty Somalis has gathered, shouting and jostling. The wound is hours old; air is leaking from the boy's lung under the skin around his back and down one arm. Speaking through the MEU's Somali translator, Kyllonen explains each move to the patient and the crowd as he carefully cleans the wound. Then he tapes an airtight dressing over it to keep the boy's other lung from collapsing. They strap the boy onto North's cot and load him into the Hell Bitch, crammed in among MRE boxes and water and fuel cans.

It takes three hours to get the wounded boy to the hospital in Kismayu, forty miles away. At one point they confront a Somali roadblock of burning tires. The Hell Bitch plunges through it. "We were banging on the top of the vehicle yelling, 'Get this kid to this hospital, he's gonna die!'" says North.

Kyllonen and North try to keep the boy conscious. The bouncing re-opens his wounds, and blood begins to spurt from the dressings. Kyllonen and North put on new dressings and tape them down. They hold his hand and pound on the roof.

Finally the Hell Bitch swings into the courtyard of Kismayu's Red Cross hospital, a primitive place with no screens on the doors or windows, but with good foreign and Somali doctors. "I heard later that the guy made it," says Kyllonen. "Other than this, the only serious thing I had the whole time we were in Somalia was Marines with thorns in their legs."

A few hours after the Hell Bitch reaches the hospital in Kismayu, the watch officers in the MEU's operations center aboard the *Wasp* get an emergency call: A Marine helicopter has gone down about fifty miles inland along the Juba River. A crowd of Somalis has gathered.

Within seconds, the watch officers have put out an alert for the TRAP team, a unit of Marines from Charlie Company constantly on ro-tating standby for such an operation. TRAP stands for tactical recovery of aircraft and personnel. It is one of the "prepackaged" operations for which the MEU has repeatedly planned and trained. Now, it goes like clockwork.

The TRAP team is on ten-minute alert. At a summons over the ship's 1MC, they are sprinting into formation in the hangar deck, shrug-ging into flak jackets and helmets, organizing into sticks, platoon ser-geants bellowing and swearing. Equipment piles up: spare parts for the downed helo, tool kits, metal cutters, a Jaws of Life device to pry crewmen out of the wreckage, emergency medical kits, illumination grenades, weapons. From overhead comes the whine and clatter of helos warming up.

"We need the TRAP ammo package *now!*" someone bellows.

"Got it!" a sailor screams as he wrestles with ammo boxes that have just come up the elevator from the *Wasp*'s ammunition magazines deep in the hold.

Broderick and his staff have done a quick brief, with reports on weather, intelligence (no known hostiles in the region, but it's getting dark), available assets (TRAP team is good to go; so are two CH-46 helos). They have considered and approved Broderick's intent for the mission:

CH-53 passes a supply ship.

"With a minimum-size force, maximum speed and security, conduct the TRAP with emphasis on low threat posture."

The eighteen Marines hurtle out onto the flight deck to board the helos. Mark Toal watches anxiously, slapping each man on the rump as he sprints by. Toal is not going along; he would only take up extra space on the helo. But this is where Toal's stewardship of Charlie Company is tested: If he has motivated and trained these men right, they will perform

Will Hartzell, MEU
command center.

well without his supervision and even surmount whatever obstacles Murphy throws in.

"Good luck! Be careful out there!" he shouts.

As the helos lift off and bank into the setting sun, Toal says wistfully, "Wish I was going."

Down in the MEU's operations center, a dozen Marines man radio-telephones. The chief watch officer, Warrant Officer Will Hartzell, watches on a closed-circuit TV screen as the helos take off. He takes a call from the flight deck and directs a young Marine to log in on the wall chart that the TRAP team departed at 1821 hours.

Then, silence. Hartzell paces. At 1851 comes a call: Seahawks. The TRAP team has landed and is going to work on the downed helo. No injuries. Preliminary assessment is that they can get this bird to fly.

Sixty-four minutes later comes a radio burst from the ground. The downed helo is operational. The TRAP team is Yankees (extracted successfully). Hartzell grins, logs in the information, and heads down the passageway to the wardroom to make himself a cup of tea.

Lieutenant Larry Gill inspects his men's weapons.

The Marines of the 24th MEU were scheduled to pull out of Somalia in late April. That they have done well is beyond doubt. Alpha Company has been patrolling the streets of Kismayu for almost a month. They are universally liked: When they leave, they are presented with a live goat and a formal petition asking them to stay.

Yet among the Marines there is a growing conviction that such effects are only temporary. "We are treading water," said one of Broderick's officers, "and when we stop, this whole operation will sink without a trace of our ever having been here."

That is the view from the field. Up at headquarters in Mogadishu, the combined U.S./UN command is being visited by a stream of congressmen wearing appropriately grim faces and flak jackets for their one-day visits. For them, headquarters had assembled statistics to show that the huge U.S.-led intervention (at its peak, the operation boasted 38,301 troops) was working.

For instance in Bardera, one of the towns hardest hit by war and famine, the daily death rate dropped from more than three hundred in November to fewer than five in April. In Mogadishu, weapons searches and confiscations forced up the street price of an AK-47, the nearly indestructible Russian assault rifle, from under fifty dollars to almost a thousand. Probably as a consequence, the number of daily gunshot victims admitted to Mogadishu hospitals fell from about fifty to five or less, according to headquarters' statistics.

Buoyed by such rosy numbers, the U.S. military command that had overseen the UN-backed military intervention in Somalia in December 1992 was handing control over to the UN itself. Troops from Pakistan, Egypt, and Botswana were taking over checkpoints from Marines and U.S. Army troopers. It was building into the largest UN peacekeeping operation in history.

Lieutenant General Robert B. Johnston, the overall commander of U.S. forces in Somalia, flew home with a contingent of Marines. He had been given the difficult task the previous December of managing the U.S. intervention in Somalia and halting the starvation. That has been done. Johnston was invited to appear at the White House where he received the Defense Distinguished Service Medal.

"Our mission is accomplished," Johnston said, declaring the U.S. intervention in Somalia "a complete success."

This news was received with some cynicism at Camp Lejeune, N.C., where the wives of the 24th MEU were chewing their nails over the safety of their husbands in Somalia.

But Johnston's assessment was received gratefully in Washington, where a new administration had been inaugurated with a popular mandate to concentrate on domestic rather than foreign problems. ("It's the economy, stupid!" said an oft-quoted sign in candidate Bill Clinton's campaign offices.) No one wanted to hear that there might be lingering problems in Somalia.

At the Pentagon, Defense Secretary Les Aspin was trying to forge a new national security strategy to guide the armed services into the new, post–Cold War era. The new strategy was being built around "regional contingencies" like Somalia, but Somalia itself—and the U.S. forces there—were not receiving a lot of attention. Somalia, Aspin would explain later, was the fault of the Bush administration.

"Basically, the U.S. government went in there with the desire to feed the people, to avert starvation. And it did that. Then the question was, can you get out without the situation reverting to the status quo ante [civil war and starvation]? That was the question that was never answered by the previous administration."

And there was nothing the U.S. government could do—it was just stuck there?

"The situation was stuck," Aspin said.

If the Pentagon had no exit strategy for Somalia, the politicians on Capitol Hill did, a four-word strategy: Bring the boys home! (A subset of that strategy read, "Foist Somalia off on the UN.") Already, politicians were gearing up for the next intervention: Bosnia. The Clinton administration was under heavy pressure (from some of the same politicians who urged intervention in Somalia) to dispatch troops to the shattered states of the former Yugoslavia. Clinton had half promised to send troops eventually; meanwhile, the White House was urging air strikes as a less risky alternative.

If, in April of 1993, there was anybody vocally concerned about what would happen next in Somalia, he did not occupy a seat of power in the capital.

In late April, the *Wasp* battle group collected its Marines from various parts of Somalia and put to sea, heading northeast toward the Arabian Sea and the Persian Gulf where the MEU was scheduled to hold exercises with Saudi Arabia, Kuwait, and other gulf states.

These bilateral exercises are usually the meat of a MEU mission: They are intended both to flatter countries with U.S. attention and to accustom their military forces to working with Marine ground and air forces.

Before the MEU's 2,100 Marines left, they promised to be on a short "tether" to the UN: If needed, they could be back in five days.

From a windswept hilltop overlooking Mogadishu at twilight, the lights of the Marines' ships could be seen winking out as they dipped over the horizon. At night, Mogadishu is black. Except for a few lights powered by generators—at the U.S.-guarded seaport, at the military compounds at the airport, and up here at the UN headquarters—the city pulsates in foreboding darkness. A gunshot occasionally ripples through the air.

From UN headquarters on this hilltop in the late spring of 1993, the future seemed promising. Mogadishu was relatively calm, and so was the rest of the country. Most of the U.S. troops had been sent home, as promised. A twenty-nation force of twenty-eight thousand peacekeeping troops had taken over. A summit meeting had produced the agreement of the warlords on a new national government of "reconciliation" scheduled to take over by midsummer.

In New York the U.S. ambassador to the United Nations, Madeleine Albright, celebrated the UN's assumption of responsibility in Somalia as "an unprecedented enterprise aimed at nothing less than the restoration of an entire country as a proud, functioning, and viable member of the community of nations." For an organization whose leader, Secretary-General Boutros Boutros-Ghali, had been jeered and stoned by mobs in Mogadishu in January 1993, it was quite an undertaking. The UN had never before attempted anything like it.

The immediate expression of this noble purpose, however, was construction.

Through the spring and early summer, Mogadishu vibrated to the sound of bulldozers, welding torches, and giant cement mixers. It was a new city arising on the rubble of the old, a multibillion-dollar enterprise designed for the ease and comfort of the United Nations. The United States would be assessed about one-third of the cost.

At the sprawling UN compound high on its hill, and at its satellite compound at the wrecked international airport, roads were being built, sewer and water lines installed, electric power cables strung, and white, air-conditioned modular buildings hoisted into place by giant cranes.

Mogadishu was coming to resemble Da Nang of 1965, one of the fortress bases from which the U.S. fought the Vietnam War. In Somalia, the UN seemed to have brought the same bravado and damn-the-cost ambition to its mission as the Pentagon did in its Vietnam buildup. Here, as in the South Vietnam of the late 1960s, ten-foot-high concrete walls and coils of razor wire girded the protective enclaves to keep out terrorists, street urchins, and the merely curious. Adjoining buildings were demolished and their rubble carted away in an attempt to deny sanctuary to snipers.

At one end of the two-mile-long airport runway, behemoth cargo planes disgorged thousands of pallets of bottled water, plumbing supplies, satellite dishes, diesel fuel, and watermelons. As U.S. helicopter gunships lifted off and clattered away over the city, white executive jets emblazoned with the UN logo whisked away UN officials for consultations and recreation in Nairobi, two hours away. (The Mogadishu-Nairobi flights were so frequent that the United Nations maintained its own check-in counter at Nairobi's international airport, where it issued its own distinctive blue UN boarding cards and luggage tags.) One flight brought in a four-man team of American plumbers, hired to replace two thousand leaky faucets that had been installed the previous month.

For Somalis living in Mogadishu, there was no running water.

Fleets of new white Jeeps ferried UN officials around to check on the work of an army of such civilian workers. One American construction supervisor here pulled down nine thousand dollars a month tax-free. In addition to salary, civilians working for the UN or other governments here got a daily allowance of one hundred and seventy dollars to pay their hotel bills. That's thirty-five dollars a day more than they get in Paris— and Mogadishu has no hotels to speak of.

The Marines assigned to Somalia, in contrast, received one hundred and fifty dollars a month in "danger pay."

Many of the foreign civilians working in Somalia were employed by Brown & Root Inc., a Houston-based international engineering and construction firm with annual revenues of $3.5 billion. Under a "cost-plus" contract negotiated and managed by the U.S. Army Corps of Engineers, the firm was paid for its costs plus an incentive fee, or profit, of up to 9 percent. The median 1992 profit of *Fortune* 500 corporations was 2.4 percent.

The UN would spend about $1.9 billion here in 1993, most of it on construction and the maintenance of its peacekeeping troops. Less than one-third of that money was earmarked for development assistance to help Somalia "get back on its feet."

Outside the wire, as Marines refer to the Somalia beyond the UN's protective coils of razor wire, things were seething.

UN peacekeepers faced a large, well-armed, and hostile Somali population, in which every person over the age of fifteen carries at least one weapon, according to a U.S. intelligence estimate (the street price of weapons notwithstanding).

The outgoing U.S. military command in Somalia, headed by Lieutenant General Johnston, had won a long argument with the UN over who should disarm Somalia. Johnston had argued that this was outside the responsibility of U.S. forces. In Washington, the Bush administration backed up Johnston, passing the mission on to the UN as a "political problem," said Brent Scowcroft, Bush's national security adviser. And the Clinton administration had simply left the problem alone.

As a result, the warlords and their fighters were still fully armed.

In this spring of 1993, Somalia's most powerful warlord, Mohammed Farah Aidid, had just returned from visits to neighboring Sudan and, it was whispered at UN headquarters, Iran itself. It was rumored that Aidid had been told by fundamentalist Muslims to stir up trouble against the UN and the United States.

Aidid may have needed no urging. A military officer trained by Italy and the Soviet Union, Aidid, fifty-nine, had fought his way through Somalia's civil war to control much of the country. And as the chosen head of the country's largest subclan, the Hebri Gedir, Aidid seems to have assumed that he deserved a place in Somalia's postwar political structure. Aidid, in Somali, means "he who would not be insulted."

Yet insulted he was.

In the critical spring of 1993, as the U.S. was handing over Somalia to the UN, two veteran diplomatic troubleshooters who had sought to treat Aidid with firmness and respect were replaced by officials with a harder-line view of the warlords.

One of the departing officials was Robert Oakley. A former U.S. ambassador to Somalia and a veteran diplomatic troubleshooter, Oakley had served as special U.S. envoy to Somalia since December. Now Oakley, who had overseen the beginnings of political reconciliation among the

Somalia warlords, returned to Washington. The other veteran was Lansana Kouyate. An imposing, burly diplomat from Guinea, Kouyate was the only one at the UN's headquarters who "could shout back and forth with Aidid without either one of them losing face," said Tom Farah, a senior adviser to the UN in Mogadishu.

At the time, UN policy was to treat all the warlords equally. Neither Aidid nor any of his rivals were to be granted any special stature; the Somalis themselves were to decide who would rule their country. "We bent over backward to try to be neutral," said Scowcroft.

But the UN seems to have gone beyond neutrality. In effect, Aidid was treated as the enemy. In May, while the 24th MEU was busy in the Persian Gulf, the UN ceased regular communications with Aidid. Several times he proposed meeting regularly with top UN officials and was rebuffed, according to Farah, a professor at American University in Washington who was serving as legal adviser to the UN command at the time. The UN also rebuffed an Aidid plan for another peace conference. And when the UN took the first steps to set up an independent national police force and judicial system, it did so without consulting with Aidid.

It is true, as UN officials point out in their defense, that Aidid is no angel. In the spring of 1993, he was using his well-disciplined forces to bring military pressure against the UN's peacekeepers. A favored Aidid tactic was to gather a mob of stone-throwing women and children, knowing that even under assault, UN soldiers will hesitate to fire back. As these skirmishes grew more intense, UN officials alleged, Aidid several times ordered the gunning down of women and children of his own clan in order to show the bodies ("victims" of UN atrocities) for TV cameramen.

Even so, knowledgeable officials acknowledged that Aidid was a force to be reckoned with, and that the UN simply declined to reckon with him.

"The UN had good intentions, but is it possible to set up a police force—to set up a political structure—in a country divided into tight clan groups without consulting the major clans? I think not," said Farah.

"This was not a conspiracy against Aidid. It was a simple cock-up."

The problem wasn't that the UN command in Mogadishu was full of incompetents; it was, officials later acknowledged, that the UN had taken on too big a task with insufficient preparation.

On the second floor of the gutted U.S. embassy building, UN staff officers were simply overwhelmed by the task of trying to coordinate their twenty-eight thousand peacekeeping troops. Most of the troops had stopped doing foot patrols in the city's streets and markets that the Marines had done; it was too time-consuming and dangerous. When they ventured out, it was usually in convoys of armored personnel carriers. The friendly cops on the beat had become, instead, occupying troops.

The UN's assumption of command responsibility had ramifications at all levels. One was that the UN troops had difficulty getting supplies—ammunition, food, water, transportation—from the over-strained logistics resources of the UN. A few miles from UN headquarters, Pakistan's 1st Sind Regiment was getting only one-sixth of the drinking water the UN had promised to deliver. "A lot of my men are sick from drinking the local water," said the regiment's tall, thin commander. "It's not a good situation."

The UN also lost the valuable street intelligence that had been picked up by the Marines on foot patrol. Soldiers in armored vehicles weren't gossiping with people on the street. And what intelligence they did pick up wasn't always passed on to the Americans running the UN's intelligence operation.

On June 4, the UN began to implement its disarmament plan to try to rid the Somali capital of its guns. Aidid was not consulted or even advised. The afternoon before UN weapons raids began, the UN sent letters to several low-level clan members informing them of the disarmament plan. The first of the warlords' weapons caches was to be an Aidid warehouse adjacent to Mogadishu's radio station, which Aidid's forces had captured during the civil war. The clans opposing Aidid had previously asked the UN to take the station down.

As a result, when Pakistani troops set out in the early morning of June 5, Aidid's men were ready. A convoy of Pakistani armored personnel carriers was set upon with heavy weapons; three Pakistanis were killed outright and nine were taken prisoner after their ammunition ran out. (Two of the prisoners were later executed by their Somali captors.)

Across town another Pakistani convoy was ambushed. A Pakistani officer, Captain Syed Riaz Manzoor, attempted to cover the evacuation of his wounded men but was eventually overcome when he ran out of ammunition. When his body was recovered the next day his throat had been slit, his eyes gouged out, and he had been disemboweled. In all, twenty-four Pakistanis were killed and fifty-five wounded, including ten who were crippled for life. Two hundred Somalis were reported to have been killed or wounded in the fighting.

Within twenty-four hours, the United Nations Security Council in New York had unaminously demanded "the arrest, prosecution, and trial" of the perpetrators of the ambushes. Aidid was not named in the UN resolution, but he was the target of the manhunt that followed. The day after the ambushes, Jonathan Howe, the retired U.S. admiral who was chief UN envoy, told reporters grimly, "I would assume that he [Aidid] is behind it."

What had been a well-intentioned humanitarian effort to respond to widespread starvation had become instead an armed challenge to the United Nations.

In Washington, President Clinton was already under fire by Washington pundits. It was said he lacked the nerve to send bombers and troops to Bosnia. ("Bill Clinton's leadership . . . is a study in purpose without power," sneered the *New Yorker* magazine.) It was said that Clinton disdained the military, and an Air Force general had openly called Clinton a "draft-dodging, pot-smoking, womanizing," and "gay-loving" commander-in-chief. (The general was eventually sacked.)

Within days of the disaster in Mogadishu, Washington had sent four heavily armed gunships as the Somali capital braced for a widely anticipated UN retaliatory strike against the forces of Aidid. Some two hundred civilian relief workers fled Mogadishu, and UN peacekeeping troops remained barricaded in their headquarters.

The retaliation came swiftly. In a series of strikes beginning June 12, the four-engine gunships and missile-firing helicopters attacked and destroyed several of Aidid's arms caches, ammunition dumps, and the radio station. At least one TOW antitank missile veered off course and struck a private home, killing its occupants. In subsequent night attacks, the U.S. gunships adopted the tactic of circling the target building while painting it with a blinding searchlight and warning its occupants by loudspeaker to leave the area immediately. These warnings were followed, after a "suitable delay, by a full fusillade of 105-mm fire," according to a U.S. spokesman.

In counterretaliation for these retaliatory attacks, a mob of about one thousand Aidid supporters on June 17 surrounded a convoy of Moroccan soldiers. According to a subsequent Moroccan report, the women began tossing hand grenades into the Moroccan's vehicles, and the Moroccans were then caught in a crossfire from Aidid fighters lodged in residential buildings and a local hospital. Although the Moroccan commander was killed, the troopers hung on, returned fire, and eventually captured over one hundred Aidid soldiers. The Moroccans lost five dead. The wounded on both sides were treated at the hospital, which was equipped and manned by the Moroccan government as a gift to the people of Somalia.

On the other side of the Arabian peninsula, the 24th MEU has just begun a long-planned exercise with Kuwait when the trouble erupts in Somalia. At his regular staff meeting, Broderick tells his officers: "I want to dispel any rumors. I just talked to General [Joseph] Hoar [commander of all U.S. forces in the region] and we are not, repeat not, going back to Somalia. He wants the UN forces that are there to learn to handle this."

Shortly thereafter, Lance Corporal Matt Gimber is lying in his rack in an air-conditioned barracks in Kuwait, watching TV. Suddenly he sits up, shocked: CNN has just announced that the 24th MEU is back in Somalia. Gimber looks around wildly to confirm that he is still in Kuwait. He is, and he and his buddies get a good chuckle about the media being wrong again.

But eight hours later the MEU is frantically recalling its men and vehicles, spread out over several hundred square miles of Kuwaiti desert, back to the ship.

Jerk-ex. They are going back to the war.

The Marine Corps should be an organization basically for those who have nothing but themselves—no life, no loved ones, no self esteem. It reminds me a lot like prison. Prison being a lot better.
—Lance Corporal, Infantry

The USMC is a great provider for both its members and those it helps. And it pisses me off to hear a lot of the Marines talk about "how bad it is" and "it sucks." But if you offer these same Marines an early out [a program for early retirement], they won't take it. Stop complaining!
—Lance Corporal, Infantry

10

JERK-EX II
MOGADISHU, SOMALIA
June 1993

Hangar deck, 1300 hours. The *Wasp*'s huge elevator doors frame a section of the Mogadishu coastline, rising and slowly falling in the damp, sticky air as the *Wasp* rolls at anchor. A low bank of dirty gray cloud hovers over the city, which looks peaceful from a distance of four miles.

Inside the hangar deck, it is bedlam. Combat-loaded Marines are pouring in from the passageways. Others are hauling ammo crates off the magazine elevator and stacking them beside piles of weapons, radios, rope, water bottles. Men are bawling directions and yelling encouragement at each other. Overhead, the helos' turbine engines are whining up to full power.

At the center of the hangar deck, a dozen men wearing dark jumpsuits are struggling into black armored vests, pulling on black gloves and loading an armory of weapons including Heckler & Koch 9-mm submachine guns. Some carry heavy, short-handled hammers on their black web belts as well as canteens and ammo pouches and hanks of rope and other climbing gear. Chalked in large letters on each man's sleeve is his blood type, for quick treatment of combat wounds.

These men belong to the MEU's selective and highly trained commando team, Force Reconnaissance Assault Platoon.

They are highly trained in clandestine infiltration, high-speed "take downs" of targets such as terrorists or hostage-holders. Some of the MEU's senior officers do not possess sufficient security clearances to know precisely what they're capable of doing. Each member of the platoon is a combat diver and is jump-qualified. The entire team can "fast-rope" out of a helo and onto the ground or a rooftop in ten seconds. This platoon has done perhaps a thousand training missions together, using explosives to breach walls or doors, identifying in seconds the live "hostages" (played by off-duty Marines), and using live ammunition to riddle paper targets of terrorists.

The Force Recon team has been alerted for a mission. It will be working in tandem with specially trained helo pilots and crews and other specialists; together they are called the Maritime Special Purpose Force, or MSPF.

The mission is classified; the object of the mission is highly classified, closely held within a small circle of men aboard the *Wasp* and at the UN military command headquarters in Mogadishu.

But the mission is not hard to figure out. This is June 22, one day after the Marines have steamed back to Somalia and seventeen days after the United Nations command declared warlord Mohammed Farah Aidid an international outlaw. Snatching Aidid has become a high priority; around UN headquarters on the hill overlooking Mogadishu, officials talk as if nothing more can be done in Somalia until Aidid is removed.

The Force Recon team is commanded by Lieutenant Scott Burk, a tall, muscular twenty-eight-year-old who played professional football before joining the Marines. Like other members of Force Recon, Burk was asked personally to join. Unlike most of those invited, he made it through three days of physical and mental stress testing (80 percent wash out). Two years of intense schooling followed selection, making them "not special Marines, but Marines with special training," says Burk.

Nevertheless, Burk is viewed with awe by most young Marines. At breakfast in the officers' wardroom, enlisted Marines on mess duty bring him two plates of apple fritters, bacon, garlicky fried potatoes, and pancakes. They proudly bring him, in addition, a bowl of oatmeal, a pile of toast, and a plate of donuts.

Despite appetites like that, the men of the platoon are not supermen. Excepting Burk, they are not physically imposing; in civilian attire they could disappear among the crowds on any college campus. They do seem to share three traits: They are quiet, they are risk-takers, and they are tough.

An experience Burk had a year ago will illustrate. He was in a military transport plane preparing for a practice jump. He was standing on line with a dozen other men waiting for word to fling himself out the gaping rear ramp. Aside from their main and reserve chutes, the men wore heavy combat packs on their chests and weapons strapped to their legs. As the plane neared the drop zone, the jump was called off because of high ground winds. Another plane in the formation suddenly veered in front of Burk's plane; his pilot banked up sharply to avoid a collision.

And eight hundred feet over the sunbaked plains of Texas, Burk tumbled out into thin air in a spinning knot of men, chutes, weapons, and flailing limbs. One man's chute opened and was instantly shredded by the weight of the plummeting men. Burk struggled and tumbled. His main chute ripped away from him as the ground rushed up. In the final seconds, Burk yanked the rip cord of his reserve chute. Nothing. Then, *wham!*

"I hit the deck at about eighty miles an hour. Made an eighteen-inch dent in the ground," Burk says. The weapons strapped to his legs probably kept his legs from shattering, but Burk crawled away with two cracked vertebrae and a daunting list of other injuries. A short time before his doctors felt comfortable with the idea, Burk went back to jumping. He has not told this story to many people. Burk is not a bragging kind of guy.

On the *Wasp*'s hangar deck, alongside Burk's platoon, Marines from Charlie Company are also getting ready to launch.

Some are formed into the TRAP team, poised to spring into action if a helo goes down in Mogadishu. Others belong to the Sparrowhawk team, a larger number of Marines who will stand by in case Burk's men run into trouble and need quick reinforcement. As in every exercise and "real-world" operation, Broderick has all the Murphys covered. There are backups to the backups. If Sparrowhawk gets in trouble, a larger team of Marines (and another set of helos and crews) is on standby to launch. In the worst case, Broderick is prepared to put ashore every vehicle, every helo, every gun, and every Marine—cooks, computer technicians, and flight-deck hands—each of whom, after all, is a trained Marine rifleman.

With a flurry of shouted, last-minute instructions, Burk's platoon is launched. The Sparrowhawk team sprints up to the flight deck after them. Envious Marines watch them go.

"Go get 'em, girls," calls out a Marine bystander.

"Okay, let's kill the women and rape the horses!" yells a Sparrowhawk Marine with forced bravado.

"This isn't gonna be easy," a buddy admonishes him.

The troop-carrying helos and the MEU's Cobra gunships spiral away. Then, silence. The *Wasp* gently rises and falls in a blue, white-capped sea.

Cobra attack helo lifts off.

Mogadishu's battered skyline looks peaceful. The ship's brig is manned and ready to receive prisoners. People talk in whispers. Broderick paces.

Eventually comes a terse radio message, and minutes later the helos bearing Burk's platoon materialize as tiny dots and drone in toward *Wasp*'s flight deck. From a military point of view, the mission has gone flawlessly. But the target has narrowly eluded capture.

As the disspirited Marines come down the ramps of their helos, however, they are unaware that the operation has touched off a diplomatic storm. The assault has taken place in a Mogadishu neighborhood assigned by the UN to Italian peacekeepers. They had not been informed beforehand of the highly secret operation.

The Italian military commander, General Bruno Loi, is incensed. "My freedom to act in the sector under my jurisdiction in the manner I deem most appropriate has been challenged!" Loi yells at the UN command in a phone conversation, according to a correspondent for the Italian newspaper *Corriere Della Sera*.

Loi's sputtering outrage, amplified by frenetic diplomatic cables, rat-

CH-46 helos angle in toward *Wasp*.

tles the windows at UN headquarters in New York and at the White House in Washington. This is a critical moment for the United Nations, which is already shoulder-deep in its largest peacekeeping operation and standing at the possible threshold of a new era of international security.

Up to this point, the military forces under UN command have been cobbled together by compromise and artifice. Officially, the UN command is in charge. In reality, each national military commander has operated in his own way in his own sector. In essence, the UN's twenty-eight-nation peacekeeping forces are waging twenty-eight separate operations, with little or no coordination at the top. And each military commander is

backed up by politicians at home who are unwilling to cede real authority to the UN.

On the U.S. side, no one will acknowledge that the Marine operation took place or who the "target" was. American reporters in Mogadishu who saw the helos swoop in are told it was an exercise.

But *Corriere Della Sera* blows that cover. The Milan daily reports that the Marines were "hunting for Aidid." The story, which calls the incident "terribly embarrassing" and one "bound to have consequences," indeed causes a sensation.

In New York and Washington, the Italian protests are heard respectfully. Politicians nod in agreement. The Americans must be restrained. The Marines' highly trained team will not be used again in Somalia.

As Mogadishu slides into full-scale conflict, Aidid senses a shift in UN resolve and pushes his advantage. Within days his fighters ambush and kill three Italian soldiers. Several Somalis employed by the UN are shot and killed. Two U.S. soldiers are wounded when a rocket-propelled grenade is fired at their Mogadishu guard post.

Now the UN decides that Aidid should be a military target after all. "We won't be back to normal until Aidid is arrested," says Jonathan Howe, the chief UN envoy in Somalia. "It would be better if he were behind bars now."

But military intelligence reports that Aidid, now alerted that the UN might be serious about hunting him down, has begun surrounding himself with women and children wherever he goes. It will take brute force to get him, the UN command decides, and not just the stealth of a Marine snatch team.

In early July, U.S. Army attack helicopters lead a raid on Aidid's command center, blasting it into rubble. More than a dozen Somalis are killed; Aidid is not among them. In response, a crowd gathers at the site and chases down and kills four western journalists invited to see the carnage. The UN's fortress headquarters comes under heavy nightly assaults by mortars and rocket-propelled grenades.

By midsummer, most of the UN's peacekeeping troops have withdrawn inside heavily protected enclaves. No one is patrolling the streets, except for occasional armed convoys. On August 8, one of these vehicles is incinerated when it drives over a land mine detonated by Somalis hidden nearby. Its occupants, four young American soldiers, are killed instantly. In Washington, President Clinton vows "appropriate" military retaliation.

In New York, the UN's senior peacekeeping official calls together the ambassadors of a half dozen countries with more than one thousand troops in Somalia. He requests that they stop issuing orders to their troops that are contrary to orders issued by the UN command in Mogadishu. Italy demands that all combat operations in Somalia be halted; failing that, it says, it will move its troops to safer territory beyond Mogadishu.

Through the summer and late fall, Mogadishu will slide further into bloody chaos. In late August, the Pentagon will decide to send four hundred Army Ranger commandos to hunt down Aidid. By this time the Somali warlord is practiced in the art of evasion. The Rangers, given what may be an impossible mission, fail and fail again. Soon they are the butt of international scorn. ("Elite U.S. Rangers Blunder Again in Search for Aidid," trumpets the London *Times* in mid-September. "The American forces embarrass themselves in a futile exercise.")

A few days later, the Ranger force meets what appears to be a well-set ambush during an attempt to capture Aidid. Reinforcements aren't readily available; eighteen Americans are killed and seventy-seven wounded. The bodies of some American dead are dragged through the streets and one of the wounded, Chief Warrant Officer Michael Durant, is taken hostage.

In response, Clinton dispatches 5,300 more troops, igniting an uproar of protest in Congress and an escalating political battle over presidential authority to use military force.

"We could have prevented all of this and saved hundreds of lives if we'd been allowed to do our job," says one of the Marines involved in the MEU's aborted "snatch" operation in late June. "We had the capability to do the mission, and he was clearly unprepared for us; it wasn't until later on that he started getting smart about staying out of sight."

This Marine, speaking privately, says he will always feel keenly the deaths of those Americans who were killed in Mogadishu in the summer and fall of 1993.

"We could have prevented all that," he says softly, smacking a fist into his palm. "We could have prevented it."

Months later, in September 1993, I asked the Joint Chiefs of Staff to explain why the Marines had been called off from the hunt for Aidid. By this time, fault-finding and political back-stabbing over the failure of the whole intervention in Somalia had politicians and senior military officers alike scurrying for cover. After weeks of silence, the Joint Chiefs authorized a spokesman to convey this answer:

"What you saw happen, did not take place."

The same air of surrealism hangs over the MEU's final weeks in Somalia, in late June and early July. The Marines had been rushed back to Somalia to help bolster the UN's peacekeepers. Now that they're here, the UN doesn't quite know what to do with them.

In Washington, there is concern at the political impact of having the

Marines storm ashore to "save" the UN. Washington wants the UN to learn how to handle the delicate peacekeeping mission.

"When they called us back here from Kuwait I was giggling like a kid, I was singing and dancing up the passageways," Broderick, the MEU commander, says in late June. "Then to be told, 'just sit and wait,' well, it's kind of a kick in the rear end.

"But this is the first full-blown UN peace-making operation and there is a lot of learning involved, a lot of things to work out," Broderick says. "We were brought in to doubly ensure that things were going to go right. But if we were to go ashore with a big footprint, that doesn't help the UN—it would kind of show the UN can't handle it. And the UN is handling it," he says.

"So we're doing what we sometimes get paid to do—to just sit around and wait." But it's hard, he acknowledges. "I sit up here in this office, it's kinda palatial [Broderick's office, in fact, is about eight feet by ten feet with a large conference table]. But those poor Marines down there, just sitting below decks doing nothing, that's a lot to ask of a nineteen-year-old kid. They just want to go do what they're trained to do."

Actually, Broderick isn't just sitting around and waiting for something to do. He is pestering the UN command with ideas and suggestions. In his daily staff meeting, Broderick passes out a list of proposed operations and a tentative schedule. Most of them involve reconnaissance or a weapons sweep of villages and towns well outside Mogadishu; the idea is to use the MEU's helos to leapfrog well inland to keep an eye on the rest of the country. One after another, Broderick's proposals are shot down "due to political sensitivities," the MEU logbook reads.

In late June, Broderick gets permission to send two of his ships, the *Nashville* and *Barnstable County*, south to Kismayu for peacekeeping operations. Two separate operations are planned in exhaustive detail. A reconnaissance party is put ashore. The grunts are readied and helos loaded.

Just before the scheduled launch, an order is flashed to the MEU to cancel the operations. Broderick gets the word in the middle of a staff meeting. His neck fires up to brick-red and on into purple. Tight-lipped, he orders the message relayed south: recover the reconnaissance teams, steam north to rejoin the *Wasp*.

If Broderick has been given a reason for the cancel order, he doesn't share it.

Jerk-ex.

Here at anchor sits the 24th Marine Expeditionary Unit, manned and trained and equipped for combat. Ashore, people are being killed. American troops are even being picked off by snipers at the international airport, where the *Wasp*'s helicopters pick up mail and drop off passengers.

Feeling somewhat useless, the Marines' tempers fray.

Major Mike Dick, the operations officer for the infantry battalion that provides the bulk of Marines for the MEU, comes by Mark Toal's stateroom late one night. He wants to make sure that Charlie Company's Sparrowhawk team is standing by twenty-four hours a day in case U.S. troops in the city need reinforcements. The readiness of Sparrowhawk, of course, has already been checked and discussed and rechecked a hundred times.

"Keep those guys on a short string, I don't give a shit what anybody tells you," says Dick, a short, no-nonsense Marine with cropped graying hair.

He stands in Toal's doorway in shorts and shower thongs.

"What kinda string they got you on?"

"Sir, one hour," says Toal.

Jose Rocha.

"Plan on thirty minutes," says Dick, meaning that he wants Sparrow-hawk in the air thirty minutes after reinforcements are requested. "If they send for you, they needed you thirty minutes ago."

Toal, who is lying on his rack propped up on one elbow, says, "We're on the helos in thirty minutes, sir, but the platoon leaders need time to brief."

Dick says, "Do your briefings in the air. Have your canteens full, all that shit."

"Already done, sir," answers Toal.

Dick nods and leaves, saying over his shoulder, "You go half-naked or whatever, but you go."

When the door slams, Toal lies for a minute with his eyes closed. Then he jackknifes out of bed and picks up his phone.

"Hey, is Lieutenant Harrison there?" he says, asking for his Sparrow-hawk commander. "Thanks. . . . Hey, Tex, we have flashlights on our gear list, right? . . . Yeah, Okay, I thought so. Thanks."

Toal hangs up, leaps up into his rack and lies down, staring at the ceiling, his mind racing over a million details.

Tension is rising for the idle enlisted Marines as well. Jose Rocha works it off pumping iron. The ship's one-page daily newsletter, the *Wasp Wing*, details the day's reruns of weather and videos: 1600 *Oprah*, 1700 *Wheel of Fortune*, 1800 *Three Ninjas*. Weather: mostly cloudy, winds southerly five to fifteen knots, seas two to five feet, high seventy-eight degrees.

Down in enlisted berthing, Marines have hooked up a videotape player and are crammed together watching Tori Welles perform in an X-rated movie, *Chameleon*. Many other Marines are watching the drab So-mali coastline from the starboard gallery rail, a catwalk suspended about three stories above the water. It is one of the few places on the *Wasp* where Marines are allowed to smoke.

"I'm tired of this ship and I'm tired of looking at the coastline," says Matt Gimber, a twenty-two-year-old lance corporal from Lancaster, Pa. "I'm tired of looking at the water." He flicks a Marlboro butt on a long smoking arc into the waves. "I just wanna go home," he says with finality.

Broderick, aware of such rising sentiments, finally wins UN approval for two operations that write a coda to the Marines' experience in Somalia.

One is a day-long medical and dental clinic that the Marines hold in a shot-up police station in the town of Merca, forty miles south of Mo-gadishu.

The town was founded centuries ago as an Arab trading post. It has changed little. A high crenellated wall of mottled gray masonry, reminiscent of medieval European castles, protects the town from the heaving aquamarine sea. Merca's stained and crumbling buildings, crowding close upon narrow alleyways, march halfway up the side of a hill of sullen red that reflects dully on the low gray clouds overhead.

While a Marine security force fans out to discourage snipers, two Marine doctors and eight Navy corpsmen assigned to the MEU set up a table under a tarpaulin and begin laboriously logging in patients' names, ages, and complaints. One by one the patients—mostly mothers with children, and elderly men—are led into the former police station, a concrete room about twenty feet long and twenty wide. The room is bare of furniture and decoration.

The medical team, led by Lieutenant Chris Bashore, the MEU surgeon, brings along several footlockers of medical instruments and medicine. At a makeshift table, a corpsman sets up his pharmacy. In one corner, dental corpsman James Channell is using huge pliers to remove a tooth from an elderly Somali. The man, ragged and unshaven, has had a shot of Novocain, and he sits stoically as Channell yanks and twists and grunts. Another corpsman waves away flies and wipes sweat off Channell's forehead.

In another corner, Doc Bashore is listening intently as a translator explains that the woman and child seated in front of him are both in pain. The child, two-year-old Ibrahim Habib Nur, has diarrhea and bloody stools. His mother, who gives her name as Faduma Hassan Omar, wears a blinding white gown. She is twenty-two. She complains of a pain in her heart. It is difficult to know if she is speaking of angina or, more metaphorically, of a husband who has disappeared in the war.

"Okay, let's do a CAT scan," Bashore jokes in a loud voice.

He strokes the child, who looks at him solemnly with huge brown eyes. Flies gather at the corners of the child's mouth.

"He looks okay, but make sure he gets lots of fluids," Bashore tells the woman through his translator. "I'll give him some water now, and some vitamins." He examines the mother, listening to her heart with his stethoscope. She looks anemic, but without sophisticated tests there is little Bashore can do.

He gets a bottle of vitamins and carefully explains the proper dosage to the mother. He teaches her how to use the child-proof cap. He smiles at the child and strokes his head. He clasps the mother's hand and flashes her a confident, friendly smile.

Throughout the day, the medical team sees patients at a rate of thir-

Matt Gimber.

ty an hour. They treat eye infections and stomach ache, back pain and abcessed teeth, coughs, diarrhea, and dengue fever, yellow fever, malaria, scabies, and tuberculosis. Communications is difficult, even with translators, but the sparkling eyes and formal bows of the patients as they leave speak volumes about their gratitude.

At the end of the long day, the medical and security teams get a truck ride back to the landing zone where a *Wasp* helo will pick them up.

On the way out of town they ride past a long, low wall. A message is painted on the wall in neat letters:

"Well come Merca we are victims of war help help help help help."

A few days later, Broderick lands virtually his entire infantry and artillery force ashore for four days of training in an area of several dozen square miles that has been carefully scouted for Somalis. There are none. The Marines and their gear are shuttled ashore by helo. They form up into platoons and head off into the bush, each man loaded with seventy pounds of weapons, ammo, water, and other gear.

For twenty minutes every hour, it pours torrents of rain. Then the sun comes out and steams everything half-dry. The Marines are cold, wet, sandy, and sunburned. They mount night patrols and platoon-on-platoon ambushes. They set up ranges for mortars and machine guns. Flares and explosions rock the night sky.

In four days, the Marines fire off eight tons of ammunition. At the end of it, the sun comes out, and the Marines, wet and sandy and exhausted and satisfied, form up at the LZ to ride back to the *Wasp*.

QUESTION: *What do you think the 24th MEU was able to accomplish in Somalia?*

I don't think we accomplished much. . . . We were able to feed the hungry and make living better for the Somalians for the brief time we were there.
—Lance Corporal, Aircraft Technician

Nothing . . . our efforts were pointless. . . . If anything we made things worse by giving the people a brief sense of false hope. Once we pulled out things went back to the way they were before.
—Lance Corporal. Light Armored Vehicle Mechanic

I do feel that the U.S. has somewhat of an obligation to assist other countries, to a degree. I do not feel that we should involve our country in another's internal civil war.
—Sergeant Major

11

LIBBO
TOULON, FRANCE
July 1993

In the final days before the 24th MEU arrives for liberty on the French Mediterranean coast, the Marines cash $220,000 worth of personal checks at the *Wasp*'s dispersing office and change an additional $55,000 into French francs.

It has been almost five months since the Marines left Camp Lejeune; eighty days since the MEU finished up a four-day port visit in the United Arab Emirates, a liberty which in that straitlaced land hardly counted as liberty.

For almost three months, the Marines have been putting on boots and utilities every morning when they get up. They've been getting up early every day (on special Sundays, they are allowed to sleep in until seven A.M.). And when they're up, they've been confined inside a warship or running for cover someplace in Somalia.

Now they are ready to blow off some steam.

So when Broderick lets his men ashore in the picturesque port city of Toulon, it is with the expression of a player of Russian roulette gingerly pulling the trigger. He hopes nothing will go wrong.

Actually, Broderick is doing more than hoping. He is making damn sure nothing is going to go wrong. He has beat this into his lieutenant colonels, who have beat it into their majors and captains, who have put it into slightly less polite language and passed it down through their company first sergeants and platoon sergeants and squad leaders: don't fuck up.

The rules are more explicit. For lance corporals and lower ranks, liberty expires at 0200 (two A.M.). Others can stay out later and permission may be given for overnight absences from the ship. The buddy system is mandatory at all times. Anyone found without a buddy is in big trouble. Anyone leaving his buddy alone is in bigger trouble. Nobody's allowed to rent a car or motorcycle without the colonel's permission. No drinking on the sidewalks. No rowdy behavior. Marines are the guests of the French people and are to behave as guests at all times.

The off-ship dress code is detailed. Shirts must have collars and sleeves (tank tops and T-shirts are not permitted). Beach attire may not be worn to and from the ship. Shirts with pictures or writing on them must be in good taste. No frayed clothing of any sort is allowed.

Marines also get the standard lectures on drugs and sexually transmitted diseases. The STD lecture is supplemented by full-color slides that the MEU's medical officers have recently obtained. They show patients horribly disfigured by syphilis and herpes. The slides help hold down the usual jeering during the mandatory lectures.

Broderick also has press-ganged some of his officers and senior enlisted men to roam the town as "courtesy patrols" to keep an eye on things; they will augment the Navy shore patrol, the hard-eyed cops who've been the bane of Marines on liberty since the days of sail.

Liberty is an important part of Broderick's work-hard, play-hard philosophy of life. "We spend a lot of time making sure the guys don't destroy things during liberty," he says. "But the kids have worked hard and done well. They've earned this."

Military discipline, during liberty, is relaxed only slightly. Young Marines on duty may be professional and responsible beyond their years; off duty is something else. "One of the best machine gunners I have, I'd trust with my life," says Mark Toal, Charlie Company's commander. "But I don't know if I'd trust him in a bar with my sister."

The rules are not made to be broken. Already there are a handful of Marines, including some young officers, on "restriction" for breaking the rules during the last liberty port. Some must be in before dark; others are allowed off the ship only in the company of a senior Marine. A few are restricted to the ship.

At the last liberty port, a Marine beat up a local cab driver. The Marine was quickly court-martialed and got six-six and a kick—six months confinement, six months forfeiture of pay, and a dishonorable discharge.

"Okay guys, you've seen all the rules and you know what to do and what not to do out there," says Captain Joel McBroom. He is having a final talk with members of the weapons company before they gallop off the ship.

"I just have three words for you," McBroom says, and he leads them in a recitation of Broderick's catechism: "Don't. Fuck. Up."

That said, two thousand men heave off their helmets and flak jackets and boots and inhibitions and sour memories of Somalia's misery, and flood down the *Wasp*'s "brow," or gangplank. They wear floppy shorts and basketball shoes and shirts (with collars) of the most gaudy colors (rebellion against their drab fatigues) and wear their baseball caps on backward. They flow along the pier like a crazed river that's jumped its banks, and they burst out the gates of Toulon's French navy base into town, dragging sightseers and single women in their wake. While small rivulets eddy up around fast-food stands and beer joints, the main stream thunders directly toward the lissome bodies and jiggling flesh of Toulon's famed topless beach.

The Marines draw up abruptly at the sand's edge.

For weeks they have been drooling at the prospect of hanging out on a topless beach. They've been pumping iron to swell the pecs, boasting about past and future conquests, and grabbing every second of sun to tan their hard muscles. Now here it is, and it's suddenly more delicious and more (gulp) real than they'd imagined. Here are hundreds of nearly naked women, young and old, beefy and trim, mothers with children, even grandmothers—and dozens of giggling young girls looking up from their towels to see who's just arrived. And all of them . . . speaking French.

The men of the 24th MEU-SOC have just come from facing down the meanest gunmen in Somalia. Many of the Marines are veterans of D-Day 1991, when they pushed through heavy artillery barrages and poured over the berm into Kuwait to whip the Iraqi army. They're not about to let a little cultural barrier stop them now.

"I'm not looking for Miss Right. I'm looking for Miss Right Now!" the MEU's lothario, Lieutenant Larry Gill, says with a grin.

Soon they're thoroughly integrated into the scene. Four Marines are lying on the sand, face to face with a quartet of admiring women. Others have been invited into a volleyball game. Lance Corporal Russ Squires has met Beatrice Rozycki, a French student nurse, and she is massaging his shoulders and giggling in his ear. An admiring Marine asks if she thinks Frenchmen are really better lovers than Americans. She giggles and shrugs, but Squires boasts: "We're gonna kill that myth."

Captain Harry Bass bakes on the sand nearby. He is musing about

Russ Squires, Beatrice Rozycki, Toulon beach.

Somalia, where his Marines had charge of several square miles of rubble in Mogadishu. "The bodies in the streets, the squalor, the stink, wounded people going for months without treatment, my Marines out there with crowds pressing up against them. . . . It was pretty high stress," he says.

But Bass has learned that his men qualify for neither combat nor humanitarian service medals for duty in Somalia. "So what was it we were doing there?" he wonders. Then he turns over to admire a well-endowed passerby. "Aaaarrrrrgh," he growls, picking up his camera. "For me, sitting on a topless beach on the Riviera is reward enough. This is good to go!"

After dusk, the Marines drift into town. Most end up on Toulon's Rue Bon Pasteur. It is a crooked, narrow street—an alley, really—several blocks long, lined with seedy sex shops and open-front bars like Kiss Me and Play Boy.

Bar girls congregate in doorways. In front of the Hong Kong bar, a girl in a tight dress strokes her breasts and pouts at the passing Marines. Next door a blowsy blonde has her arm around a Marine dazed and weaving with drink. She is giggling and fondling his crotch. It will cost a Marine corporal about three days' wages to buy one of these girls a drink. They are lining up to do so. Jammed into the street with the Marines are more girls, weasel-faced pickpockets, occasional flying wedges of white-uniformed shore patrols, and, every hour or so, a sober-faced team of Broderick's courtesy patrol men, looking uneasily self-conscious in their crisply pressed uniforms and mirror-shined service shoes.

Over the pulsing din of rock music, a beer bottle smashes and a siren wails in the distance. To sailors and Marines the world over, this part of Toulon is known, fondly, as "the Gut."

Deep in the Gut near midnight, Danny Fish and his boys from the *Wasp*'s metal shop sit on the curb, watching the action pass and swigging beer from liter bottles. These Marines have been sweating together in the small shop fifteen hours a day for almost five months with hardly a day off. Temporarily released from that bondage, here they are drinking together.

"We get the boss drunk, then we roll 'im," says one Marine, nodding happily at Sergeant Fish. But another Marine sums up their after-hours camaraderie this way:

"We're all we've got."

The Gut.

James Channell.

Further down the curb are Chris Roupp, Scott Rogers, Tim Poupard, and James Channell. They are drinking Heineken beer from a stout supply they have cached in a duffel bag and, surprisingly enough, they're talking shop. Channell is a dental technician (it was he who was pulling teeth at the dental clinic in Merca, Somalia, a few weeks ago).

"I'm supposed to be responsible for two or three hundred Marines," he says. "Because of the cutbacks, I got twenty-five hundred guys to take care of, and that means . . ." He stops to snap a picture of a spectacularly cantilevered girl flouncing down the street. "That means that preventive dentistry is out the fuckin' window." He is about to get worked up about this, but his attention is distracted. "Awesome," he breathes beerily as a girl in a skin-tight purple miniskirt sashays past him.

Roupp, a wiry, twenty-eight-year-old sergeant, is responsible for everything that moves on or off the ship. He must know the location of every crate of water bottles, every vehicle, and every vehicle's third spare carburetor; he must get them to where they are needed (Three hundred miles into the Somali desert? In two hours? Roger that!) and must account for them when they're used or check them in when they're returned. Roupp's good-natured face is often creased with a slight frown.

"It's a hard job. If something goes wrong, it's usually not our fault but we're the ones that get chewed," he shouts over the din of the Gut. "Sometimes we do fuck up," he says, "like in Somalia, we got a message to deliver tires to the beach pronto. Remember?"

Roupp snorts with laughter and nudges Scott Rogers, who takes up the tale.

"Supply sent us up the tires okay and we got 'em ashore and they're like, 'What the fuck?' because the tires we gave 'em had no rims. We thought they came with rims," says Rogers. "So it was the supply guys' fault but we got blamed." They all chuckle and drain their bottles and reach for new ones.

"But I love it," Roupp says after a moment's silence, and his eyes are shining.

He fires up a Marlboro with his Zippo, and backs into the wall to make room for the shore patrol. It is led by Steven Smith, a Navy warrant officer. He has a beefy neck and red face and is big enough to bulldoze Marines like Roupp with his chest. At forty-six, Smith is a weary veteran of scenes like the Gut, and in his opinion, they just don't make 'em like they used to.

Smith may be suffering from Old Timer's Gripe. But he is also right.

This is not the Marine liberty enshrined in American lore by a beer-guzzling, wench-grabbing, fist-swinging John Wayne. For one thing, most Marines aren't even here in the Gut. They're off sightseeing or feasting at local restaurants.

The Marines here are drinking, sure; some of them are even stumbling. But each has a buddy, and as for the girls, by and large the Marines are just looking. When Channell puts the moves on two bar girls named Sandy and Melissa, what he wants is to have his picture taken with them. Then he's back to drinking with his buddies.

"I've seen more action in graveyards," Smith sneers as he bulldozes his way through the crowds.

"It has changed—when I joined ten years ago I did things I'm ashamed to even think about now," says Roupp. "Now, guys get drunk and look at women. Ten years ago they'd a been chasing 'em down the street.

"I think anymore people realize if you get in trouble you're out" of the Marine Corps, Roupp says. "And in this economy, the civilian world isn't as enticing a place as it used to be."

Other things have changed, too. Not long ago, heavy drinking was the way young Marines proved their manhood. In recent years, the military has cracked down on drug and alcohol abuse and on drunk driving. (One conviction is generally enough to end a military career.) Social drinking within the military has declined.

But a Pentagon-sponsored study released in 1993 showed that the Marine Corps, among all U.S. armed forces, has the largest proportion of heavy drinkers (those consuming five or more drinks a night at least once a week). The rate of heavy drinking among eighteen-to-twenty-five-year-old Marines is more than two and a half times higher than among their civilian counterparts.

Still, physical fitness has become the standard of machismo, and pumping iron is as much admired as guzzling beer. Particularly on a float, since alcohol is not allowed on ship.

Also, today's Marines are better educated than the Marines of forty or fifty years ago, and on this liberty their interests extend far beyond the Gut.

Brian Mullane, a strapping twenty-four-year-old redhead from Onstead, Mich., skips the Gut altogether. He hops a bus with his buddies and goes to Paris for two days. Mullane is a tough corporal who led combat patrols in some of Mogadishu's most dangerous neighborhoods. But in Paris, Mullane is just another gaping tourist. "The Louvre was awesome—I took four flash pictures of the Mona Lisa to make sure it comes out. We hung around the Eiffel Tower and met some American girls, stayed out until the subway closed and walked miles back to our hotel, right through the Arc of Triumph. We went everywhere and saw everything," he enthuses.

"Somalia is just bad memories now."

Mad Dog, the helo pilot, goes straight to the local Harley-Davidson motorcycle dealer. When Mad Dog was growing up in Cadiz, Ky., he didn't learn much French. But motorcycle talk transcends mere language barriers. Mad Dog hooks up with a group of French bikers. They lend him a bike and tour the countryside. One biker takes him home for dinner with the family.

Kenneth Thompson, a twenty-year-old lance corporal from Indi-

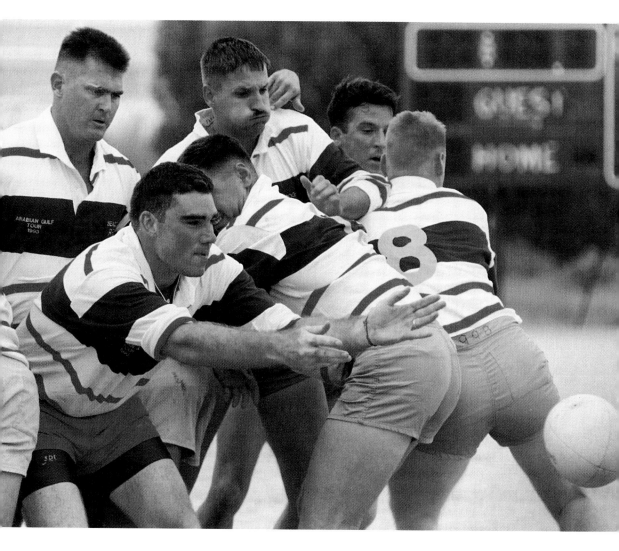

Marine rugby.

anapolis, sets up a trip down the coast to Marseilles. He and his buddies set themselves a budget and hunt down an inexpensive hotel and restaurants. They put away some beer but find time for other pursuits. "We got to see the opera house, we ate quiche and went to the cathedral, which was a hump and a half [a long walk] but worth it," says Thompson.

In a quiet neighborhood café in Toulon, Andrew Tempesta, a helo pilot from Boston, is finishing a plate of mussels steamed in butter and cream and garlic. "I sopped up this stuff with crusty bread and, oh my!" he says.

Further along the street, Joel McBroom and Corporal Joe Murphy

Donald Mortimer tours Toulon museum.

are on courtesy patrol duty. "Hookers here are hard-lookin' women," says McBroom, watching the street scene. "You'd have to be desperate. . . ." They take a break at a café and McBroom buys Murphy his first-ever espresso coffee. Murphy, from Cincinnati, is twenty-three. "Not bad after you get past the first swallow," he allows politely.

A few Marines borrow tents and go camping in the mountains above Toulon. Others go scuba diving and sailboarding off the beach. One Marine claims to have gone naked bungee jumping.

Broderick is not having so much fun. One day he and his executive officer, Butch Preston, tour a local French army live-fire range to see if it would be suitable for the Marines to use on a future float. The next day, Broderick has formal meetings with Toulon's mayor and police chief, and a French commodore.

Classic grip 'n' grin-ex.

Now Broderick sits in his stateroom, signing letters that will accompany the *Wasp* baseball caps and engraved Zippo lighters that are given as gifts to the local dignitaries.

Broderick is in a rare introspective mood. The ship is quiet. The stress of Somalia is behind him. Ahead lies home. Thoughts of retirement intrude on his work. He has always said he will go do something else when he stops having fun in the Marine Corps. Somalia was difficult, but it was fun. Just him and his Marines, and if higher authorities imposed tight limits on what he could do, he was relatively free within those constraints to apply his intelligence and guts to a very difficult situation.

Now he is up for promotion from colonel to brigadier general, a level few officers ever reach. It would be a stunning honor. It would also lift him further away from direct contact with the Marines he loves, and it would entangle him further in the bureaucracy he doesn't love.

And what would he do if he quit? "I could go back to teaching, maybe high school," he says. "But schools are getting dangerous. Hell. I could get blown away!" He chuckles.

"The other thing I've thought about . . . There's a guy at the Food Lion [supermarket] at home I kinda admire. He sits at the checkout counter eight hours a day. Name of Walter. He's got no worries, a steady income, indoor work, health and retirement plan. . . . I'd kinda like to be Walter."

Broderick will wait until the promotion list comes out at the end of the year. Plenty of time then to decide what to do. Meanwhile, these damn letters have to be finished.

While Broderick works, other Marines tend to duties, too: calling home. Brad Myers calls his girlfriend, Heather, to try to patch things up. "She has a three-year-old daughter and I missed her birthday and I was kinda sad about that," he says. "The last letter I got, she said she was thinking things over about us, because I'm here and she's there and it's kinda hard," says Myers, twenty-one. "I got bad vibes from that letter, so I wrote and said she didn't need to meet me when we get home. It kinda sounded like things were over."

But in an hour-long phone call, they rekindle their romance. "She said she wouldn't meet me if I didn't want her to but she kinda wanted to," Myers says. "We worked it out. We're back together again," he says with a huge smile.

Norm North calls home, too. His wife, Debbie, is stressed out. She has closed down their rented house in Jacksonville and moved out to Indianapolis to live with her mother. She is looking for a house to buy in Cincinnati where Norm has been assigned to recruiting duty when he gets home. Their furniture is in storage. Her parents have their own ideas about bringing up Debbie and Norm's infant daughter, Brianna.

She and Norm get into a hollering fight about something neither can quite remember later. North finally slams down the phone and skulks off in a black mood. Next night he tries again. "I said I was sorry, she said she was sorry, and we had a great talk," he says.

When Marines tire of the beach, the Gut, and the telephones, they drift over to the local office of the United Service Organization. For decades the USO has catered to homesick soldiers and sailors and Marines. It still does, here in the person of an energetic woman named Joyce Lawrence. She and her volunteers staff the center's pool rooms and video lounges, arrange tours, provide telephone service, advice, and motherly concern. It shocks her that Marines and sailors, after being cooped up on the *Wasp* with little to do for entertainment but watch TV, are slouching in her lounge watching TV. "They don't get enough of it on the ship?" she wonders.

The USO arranges a tour to the wine country of Provence. Harry Bass and Mark Toal and Mike Dick sign up and join the busload of Marines, chattering happily like kids on a school outing. They buy cases of wine, take a walking tour of the medieval town of Avignon. On the two-hour twilight ride back to the *Wasp*, they sip their Chateauneuf-du-Pape. "Maybe I'm getting old," says Toal, "but I wish my wife was here."

"I can't take too much more of this, night after night," agrees Bass. "People do get bored with libbo, yeah. It's expensive here, and also people are anxious to get home."

For a lot of Marines, liberty is a time to escape the crowds and noise of the ship. That's what Donald Duggins and Eddie Jones are doing: just sitting on a park bench, watching a mother push a stroller in the soft Mediterranean dusk and talking about nothing in particular. The two Marines had gone to Monaco, just up the coast, and checked into a $125 hotel room with three other Marines. "I forgot all the French I ever had in high school," says Jones, a forty-four-year-old warrant officer from Houston. "We went into one casino, it was glittering, man. This guy asked me to check my camera. Everybody else was driving up in Rolls and Mercedes, checking furs. I just didn't feel right, so we left," he says.

Born-again Eddie Adams has the same feeling about Toulon. He has been fighting off the temptations of pornography for five months. Now he is fighting off the temptations of drink as well. "I don't want to go out

William Devine, chaplain (left).

there. I know what I'm gonna find," he says, having heard stories of the topless beaches and the Gut.

Nevertheless, one day he pumps up his courage and sails out into Toulon. His mission, he tells himself, is to look for a new suit: He's been invited to preach at a church in Jacksonville when the MEU gets home, and Adams doesn't have a suit. He doesn't find one in Toulon. But walking through a park, he spies a couple making love in the bushes. When he goes to buy postcards, they all seem to feature naked women. Adams has a fast lunch at McDonald's, and flees back to the *Wasp*.

Chris Baron has an entirely different experience. He has been searching for a true love. Unexpectedly, he finds her. It happens in a restaurant where he is eating dinner with Marine buddies. She is with her family at a table across the room. She is French. In a voice still dazed with awe days later, Baron relates what happened. "I saw her laugh. She put her hand up over her mouth. It was the most beautiful thing I had ever seen. I don't usually do things like this, but I got up and went over and said, 'Would you smile like that for me?' And she smiled, and she said, 'Yes.'"

Chris Baron wangled a two-day pass and spent it with Alexandra. Chris likes to fish; Alexandra keeps a fishing rod in her car. They both like to hike and camp; they share a passion for chess and, Chris says, "talking about deep things—you know, the kind of things you would never talk about on the ship."

As time runs down, they pledge it won't end here. Alexandra will come visit Chris in the States in September, six weeks away.

After hours, the Marines boast of sexual conquests and disparage others' feats. Lieutenant Gill is talking about picking up chicks at a disco when someone interrupts.

"Those were men, Larry. That was a transvestite bar."

Gill's face freezes for a moment, then breaks into a grin.

"Naw," he says.

"Sure was," says another lieutenant, picking up the joke. "Din'tja see his Adam's apple? Women don't have big Adam's apples, Larry. That was a man you were dancing with."

Gill is laughing now. "Ah, fuck you guys," he says.

The story of Gill and the "transvestite bar" accelerates and circulates. In the officers' wardroom lounge a few hours later, there is idle speculation about how much romantic action certain officers have seen during liberty. Gill, coming in on the tail of the conversation, tells the room half-jokingly, "I could have gotten laid every night."

"We're talking about women, Larry," shoots back another lieutenant, and the room erupts in laughter.

But even this banter gets tiresome after a while. With home now three weeks away, the Marines start dreaming of being off the ship for good. "I'm going to sit in the backyard with the family and do a lot of nonphysical touching," says Willie Porter. "Just sitting quietly. We'll be taking a deep breath and saying, 'Thank God that's over.'"

Liberty in Toulon ends after eight days as if by common agreement. The novelty of the topless beach has worn off, the Gut has gotten tiresome, and Marines are starting to seriously run out of money.

Washdown, Rota.

And some are getting into trouble. Twenty-four more Marines are put on liberty restriction for offenses ranging from rowdiness to missing curfew. Several officers get into a drunken fight. Two Marines are brought into the sick bay to be treated for alcohol poisoning. Another drinks lighter fluid.

One night, several of Mark Toal's Charlie Company Marines stay out late and fall asleep on Toulon's beach. Toal revokes their liberty. "They understand that," he says. "They're good Marines, they are not discipline problems and they're reliable." The last couple of days Toal relents and lets them go to the beach with a sergeant.

From Toulon, the *Wasp* battle group steams through the Straits of Gibraltar and ties up at Rota, a joint U.S.-Spanish naval base. Here, every vehicle and piece of equipment is unloaded onto the pier, blasted with high-pressure water hoses, and scrubbed down to the satisfaction of inspectors for the U.S. Department of Agriculture. Once they have certified that no speck of foreign soil is left, the vehicles are loaded back on ship.

The Hell Bitch and other vehicles are parked on the pier, gleamingly clean, waiting to be inspected. "Been waiting since zero-six [6 A.M.]," says Flores, sitting unhappily in the sun. It is now five P.M.

Eddie Adams directs traffic at the brow. It is not an easy job. Vehicles are still being unloaded down the ramp. Throngs of Marines and sailors are trying to get up, or down, the same ramp. Forklift trucks are waiting to board with pallets of Bimbo brand hot dogs, lettuce, and fresh eggs.

"What a clusterfuck," grins Steve Conway. It is a grueling task that goes on twenty-four hours a day for three days.

At pierside, a U.S. military television crew arrives to interview Marines.

"And what do you do cooped up on those ships for so long?" the pretty young blond interviewer asks one Marine.

"There's this long silence," the Marine recalls later. "I'm thinking, 'Well, we jerk off until our eyes cross.' And I can't think of anything else to say. It was embarrassing."

Staff Sergeant North, the MEU's photojournalist, takes photos and stories about the MEU's operations in Somalia up to the U.S. Navy public affairs office at Rota, and hands them to Navy Lieutenant Rebecca Colonna. She is editor of the base's big-circulation newspaper. She looks at

North's material doubtfully. Somalia is no longer a story. Nobody really cares what the Marines did there.

"I don't wanna say that nobody gives a shit," Lieutenant Colonna says. "But even I don't give a shit." She hands the material back. North trudges away in angry silence.

There is barely enough time for a few hours of liberty. But it turns out that's time enough to get in trouble.

On a gray morning just before dawn, the ship's loudspeakers summon all Marines to the flight deck.

A thousand Marines grumble and stumble up to the flight deck, where platoon sergeants bellow them into formation. "What the fuck's up?" demands a Marine. This can't be a man overboard drill; the *Wasp* is

Sergeant Major Curtis Roderick oversees the lineup.

tied up at pierside. The Marines have never been called to an unscheduled formation on the flight deck.

The Marines stand uneasily, packed on the windy flight deck. Black clouds race across the dawn sky. Something has gone terribly wrong.

Broderick paces furiously before them. A crime has been committed in town the night before, he tells them. Alleged date rape. The female says her assailant is a Marine from the *Wasp*. She is here to pick him out.

At this, a shudder of foreboding and shame trembles through the ranks. Marines often skate along the edge of the Corps's discipline code. When they stray over the line, they are quietly counseled and punished. This is different, more like . . . a public hanging. The honor of the *Wasp*, the 24th MEU, the Marine Corps, has been stained, and the perpetrator will be identified in public. (And who among these Marines, carousing on the town last night, might have said or done something later misconstrued by his date?)

First, all black Marines are excused. Then all Marines with Oriental features or blond hair. Then all remaining Marines are told to take their shirts off, and those without tattoos on their backs are excused.

About 150 men are left. Slowly, they are paraded past a darkened window at the edge of the flight deck. Halfway through the line, a signal is received from inside. The MEU's strapping sergeant major, Melvin Turner, steps forward and lays a hand on a Marine's shoulder. After a brief exchange, Turner and the Marine disappear inside. The Marine will be tried by a naval court ashore, days after the *Wasp* sails. When the Marines arrive home at Camp Lejeune, he will not be among them. His career is probably over.

"I couldn't think of anybody in my company who would have done something like that," says Mark Toal. "But I was plenty nervous."

In the final hours before the *Wasp* sails, Marines stock up on gifts at the naval base exchange (Norm North buys a stuffed toy animal for his daughter, Brianna). Chris Baron gets a call through to his new girlfriend, Alexandra. It has been a week since they said good-bye. Yes, she is still planning to fly to the States to meet him in September. Baron stands in a phone booth on the pier for an hour, reluctant to hang up. Yes, she still loves him, yes. Later, a buddy asks him if he had been afraid the romance might have cooled. "It crossed my mind," he admits.

With two weeks of drab shipboard life ahead of them, the Marines stuff themselves with pizza and beer, and finally stagger back on board.

The required drill is to mount the brow, turn aft, smartly salute the flag, then salute the Navy officer of the deck and bark, "Permission to come aboard, sir!"

James Channell and his buddies, who had such a good time in the Gut in Toulon, are among the last aboard. Channell steers a determined but meandering course up the brow, fires off a lopsided salute aft, and peers in the general direction of the officer of the deck.

"Permission to cross the patio, Daddy-O!" he warbles.

The officer smiles primly and returns the salute.

The Marine Corps has drastically changed since I joined back in '81. . . . As a private and PFC, when a lance corporal or corporal told me to do something it was done no questions asked. I can remember beating some shitbird's ass in my day, but that's all changed now. If you even cuss now your career is done. It doesn't matter. I'm a Christian now and see it was all macho-type bullshit.

—Sergeant, Infantry

Chris Baron.

12

FANTAIL

USS BARNSTABLE COUNTY, MID-ATLANTIC

August 1993

On a warm, windy evening in mid-Atlantic, the USS *Barnstable County* heaves and pitches and rolls through a whitecapped sea. Shreds of purple and pink cloud tumble along the sky toward the setting sun. Gusts of wind tear words and cigarette smoke from the mouths of a dozen Marines riding the *Unstable*'s fantail, at stern of the ship.

Chow is over; they've seen the ship's small library of videos a hundred times, and for some reason known only to Marine rule-makers, they're not allowed to lie in their racks with their utilities on.

So they do what Marines always do when they have a chance. Stand around and bitch.

They start with the Marine Corps itself, of course. It's getting soft. Not like the hard old days. "Marines oughtta be real brawlers," says a swarthy staff sergeant. "Go into town and kick some butt. Now, you gotta walk on water just to stay in. It's kinda messed up."

He flicks his cigarette into the wind, which deposits it thirty yards astern in the churning wake.

"There's no real security anymore," he continues. "Take a guy who's a lance corporal. He's got no future. He can't stay in the grunt infantry, they got new kids coming up from boot camp. So he gets moved up, pushed up. He goes out to see what other [Marine Corps] jobs there are. Ya got truck driver, garbage hauler, that's about fuckin' it. So he gets out.

"Now," the staff sergeant says, coming to the point, "now ten, twenty years down the road you'll have lost all your experience because these guys are bailing out. See, your experience is going out the fuckin' window. And I'd tell any friend of mine not to come into the Marine Corps and that makes me sad."

The fantail Marines glumly watch the horizon. It goes up and down like a yo-yo.

"What pisses me off?" says another Marine. "Politicians messing around with the Marine Corps." This man is thin and wiry, with a shadow of a blond mustache on his upper lip. "Put women in the Corps. Put gays in the Corps. What's it gonna be next, fuckin' . . . ah . . . fuckin' one-armed, whatchacallit . . ."

"Albino women?" someone says.

At the mention of women, an electric current of resentment seems to jolt the crowd. Another staff sergeant: "I gotta give classes on sexual harassment because a bunch of officers fucked up in Tailhook." (He is referring to the 1991 naval association convention at which about ninety sexual assaults took place, according to the Defense Department's inspector general.)

Staff sergeant tucks in a fresh pinch of Copenhagen, works the shredded tobacco around under his lower lip, and continues.

"You chew out a Marine, okay. You chew out a WM [woman Marine] and it's sexual harassment. At inspection, you lift up a guy's blouse to check his gig line [making sure his shirt buttons and trouser fly are lined up properly]. For a WM, you have to ask, 'Can I do this?' To check for body fat, you pinch a guy's waist. You got a WM, you gotta ask permission and have witnesses.

"It's bullshit, man, it's fucked up," he says, spitting tobacco juice into the sea. "Hey Anderson! Tell 'em!"

John Hewet Anderson, a twenty-one-year-old private from southern Ohio, leaps off a packing crate lashed to the deck and staggers across the deck. He is a handsome man with thick brown hair, intelligent eyes, and a quick smile. He has obviously told this story often.

"Okay, this is when we were doing training off of Camp Lejeune before we went to Somalia? We're doing some kind of refugee drill. We got these people in a boat, they're Marines and Navy guys, remember it was cold so they've all got heavy coats on with hoods and life jackets and stuff. And we're all at the rail here, we're going to take 'em on board or whatever. And one of 'em is gesturing toward his mouth. We're all yelling back

and forth, you can't really hear anything. So I yell out, "What, you wanna suck my dick?"

It was a split-second indiscretion with the kind of crude language common at all levels of the military. And it would have passed unre-marked, except that one of the people huddled in the small boat was a female naval officer.

"Next thing, they've got everybody out of the rack that night saying

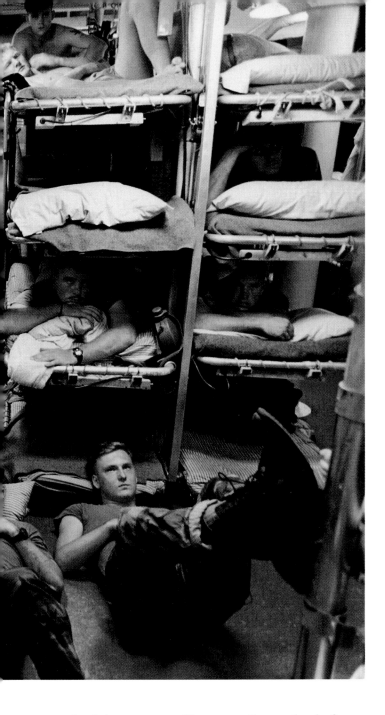

Enlisted berthing,
USS *Barnstable County*.

nobody's gonna get liberty until somebody fesses up to who said it," says Anderson. "I'm married. I like women, I don't have anything against women. This was just a stupid thing I said. If I'd known there was a woman on that boat I never would have said anything like that."

Anderson was taken off the *Barnstable County* that night by helicopter and whisked to the *Wasp* for a summary hearing. The Marines were astonished at the swiftness of the proceedings (often, these things drag out for weeks). Anderson was busted a rank, from lance corporal to private first class, and fined two hundred dollars. Worse than the immediate punishment was the long-term implication: With this blot on his record, Anderson stands little chance of being promoted. His career in the Marine Corps, he believes, is probably over.

(The senior officer on the *Wasp* who oversaw the proceedings against Anderson says the punishment was deserved. "It was poor judgment on his part," this officer said. "Sure, we use that kind of language in grab-assing all the time. But standards have changed. We do need to clean up our act.")

But it seems to the fantail crowd this evening that women are causing the trouble. Somewhere back in Washington, somebody—not a Marine!—has decided that women should have an equal place alongside men in the Corps. Okay. Nobody here has any trouble with that idea, in principle. All kinds of people compete for a place in the Corps; here on the fantail are blacks, Puerto Ricans, farm boys and ghetto boys and college boys. Maybe even a closet gay.

Trouble is, they say, women (WMs) don't compete equally. They don't have to meet the same physical fitness standards, for example: Men must complete a three-mile run, women a one-and-a-half-mile run; men must do forty sit-ups, women twenty-two. The politicians who insist that women have equality within the Marine Corps also decreed that women not be allowed to fill combat jobs. So they fill all the good, soft home-port jobs while the grunts are ripped from their families, sent into the misery of Somalia, and bounced around on the *Barnstable County*.

"I'm out here in the fleet, I've been home two years out of the last five and will stay out here because all the good [shore] jobs are filled by women because they can't deploy," says a bitter Karl Brenstuhl.

A captain, Brenstuhl is the MEU's assistant intelligence officer. "Do I want the assistant naval attache's job in Hong Kong? Sure. Do I want to be on the intel staff in London? I'd give anything for a job like that," he says. "But there's not enough guys for the fleet and too many women ashore."

The *Barnstable County* wallows in four-foot swells. Its engines rumble, and the wind whips diesel smoke and the warm exhaust from the ship's galleys (moist aroma of tonight's barbecued pork) past the knot of men on the fantail.

"Let 'em come in on an equal basis, okay," says a corporal. "Way it is now, I come in with a WM, she gets electronics school and I get infantry because there's no room in electronics school because of all the WMs in there who can't do anything else."

"I think they can do grunt work, at least some of them," a sergeant maintains. "During Desert Storm, I trained a bunch of WMs. Reservists. They didn't take baths for weeks, they didn't worry about their nails. One woman had a high and tight [haircut]. I saw her put in a chew of Red Man [tobacco], I thought she was a man. When I heard her ask a question, I said, 'Holy shit! A WM!' They did all right."

The fantail Marines approach the issue of gays much the same way.

On a personal level, homosexuality disgusts and repels them. Many Marines, in addition, hold a moral or religious objection to homosexuality. Most of all, they object to a special-interest group demanding recognition of its own special lifestyle, being wedged into an institution like the Marine Corps that has built intense pride and combat effectiveness on the principle of conformity to common standards. No special treatment for anybody.

"We never ask anybody to join," says one Marine. "You want to be part of this outfit, you gotta meet the standards. If you're a woman or a gay or a Martian, you gotta meet the standards. Otherwise, go do something else."

"The Marine Corps works fine now," says another Marine. "We go out and do this shit and we get paid all this money"—his eyes twinkle—"and it works great. Now people wanna put in women and gays. Why you wanna fuck with it?"

Grabbing the rails, the fantail Marines make way for two mess boys bearing the evening's garbage. Over the rail it goes, to a hoarse cheer.

The conversation resumes at the subject of politicians. They are the ones clamoring for gays and women to be granted a place in the Corps. What do they know?

"Who leads the military? People who've never been in the military," says a lance corporal. "The commander-in-chief has never been in the military, and that makes a big difference to me. Civilians running the military don't allow the military to be efficient. They put in women and gays. That runs down efficiency and cohesiveness.

"In Vietnam," he asserts, "a lot of Americans lost their lives because civilians were running the show. Also in Somalia. We could have done some good, if we'd been allowed to."

"They ought to give the military a mandatory vote on gays," says a Marine. "I guarantee 95 percent no. That's the way they ought to decide this, not by some bureaucrat sitting behind a mahogany desk in an air-conditioned office."

At this point a dozen Marines leap into the conversation, shouting to be heard. A burly master sergeant wins the scuffle, thanks to a foghorn voice toughened by years on the drill field. His idea brings shouts of approval.

"All politicians," he says, "should be required to serve in the military, so they know what the hell they are talking about. It oughtta be a new law: Nobody can run for anything unless they've served."

"Good evening, gentlemen!"

The sound rips across the deck like an explosion. Heads swivel. A short, plump woman stands on the deck a distance away. Like an old tar, she has planted her feet wide on the rolling deck. Her blue pants and blue-and-white polka-dot blouse snap noisily in the wind.

She grips a microphone. *"In a few weeks you men are going to be home, reuniting with your families and loved ones! This can be a time of great stress. It can also be a positive experience if you are prepared."*

On the fantail, the shock of seeing a woman on the warship has worn off. Now, the Marines know what is coming.

Return & Reunion lectures have become a recent standard of Marine Corps deployments. With reason. After six months away, Marines hit their hometown, Camp Lejeune, with even more boisterous exuberance than they hit a good libbo town like Toulon. They've been crammed below decks or on checkpoint duty in Somalia, where they've had little opportunity to spend their paychecks. Now, they're infected with consumer fever. Some succumb to temptation and blow it all in the first twenty-four hours on the stereos, cars, and cowboy boots they've been dreaming of for months. Often, the money they blow is the savings their wives have painfully accumulated for a downpayment on a washer-dryer or back-to-school clothes for the kids.

Senior officers dread the first night home, when many of their young charges burn rubber on their way toward the flashing neon of the honky-tonks along Lejeune Boulevard, Jacksonville. Worried officers insist that the rate of drunk-driving arrests and crashes rises significantly the first few nights the Marines are home. Not true, say state troopers and local police. "You got one group coming back, sure, but another

Cook William Gibson, enlisted mess, *Barnstable County.*

group's gone out. It pretty much evens out," says a Jacksonville city cop. Most alcohol-related arrests are of civilians, according to state police records.

Still, Marines do get drunk and cause accidents, and their officers worry.

"Drive safe when we get home," the MEU's infantry commander, Richard Natonski, told his men a few days ago. "We've been through a lot of shit together, we've been shot at, all kinds of things. I'd hate to see any Marine or sailor hurt or get killed in the rush."

The Marine Corps and Navy are making a studied effort to address these problems. Their solution is the woman standing here on the deck: Kathleen Morris, an education specialist from the Navy Family Service Center in Little Creek, Va. She joined the MEU during liberty, and during the long voyage home, she will conduct lectures and classes aboard the MEU's four ships. One class is called "Reestablishing Intimacy" (On the *Wasp* one night, a ship's announcement brings down the house: "All officers please muster for reestablishing intimacy on the hangar deck.")

There are other classes on dealing with teenagers and newborns, on family finances, even one on buying a new car, with tips on which unscrupulous local car dealers to avoid.

"I want all your guys to attend these classes," Broderick has instructed his officers. "Because the guy who doesn't wanna go is the one who will go back and tear the clothes off the wife without getting her wound up. He's the guy who will try to cleanse his soul by confessing the number of times he got laid on liberty, the guy who will go spend all the money she saved on a new car."

The fantail Marines are expert at sitting through lectures, at appearing attentive (eye contact!) while letting the mind wander. This one is a bit different. A break in the routine. More important, Kathleen Morris has brought along an assistant. She is Margaret Loew, a licensed clinical social worker. She is a civilian, the daughter of a naval officer. She is blond, young, and pretty. Now she takes the microphone.

"Sex is a great stress reliever!" she announces.

The fantail Marines jump to attention. A couple of officers appear on the bridge deck, leaning over the railing and drinking in the scene.

"The women are going to be real concerned about whether they are still sexually attractive. So court her before you dive right in. You might feel awkward, so talk about it," says Margaret Loew. The Marines are hanging on every word. This might get interesting.

"Let's talk about the advantages of a long-term, committed relationship—what are the advantages?" she shouts over the wind.

Silence and blank faces.

"Anybody?" she pleads.

Silence.

"Okay, I guess this is the wrong group to ask." She laughs. "AIDS, they're saying that anybody you've slept with over the past seven years, you're also sleeping with everybody they've slept with in the past seven years. So it's important to use a condom and spermicide. Everybody knows how to use a condom accurately, right?"

Silence. Marines look at their feet. In the Marines, you don't volunteer for anything. You don't put your hand up. You don't stand out. Otherwise you might get in trouble. Ms. Loew might ask you to demonstrate putting on a condom. What if you screwed up? You'd never live it down.

"I guess that's a yes," she says, handing the microphone back to Kathleen Morris.

"Okay, you guys know there's a lot of violence back home, and just because you're Marines doesn't mean you're not susceptible, so think safety!" she says. This produces some chuckles on the fantail.

"Remember, they're expecting Daddy, not Sergeant. Don't start out ordering everybody around. Your wife has been handling things, doing things her own way. Respect that. Don't take over right away. Let her drive you home the first night."

Kathleen Morris drones on. Marines on the fantail turn away to light cigarettes and gaze at the horizon.

It is almost dark now; the sun has burned below the horizon and the wind is freshening. *Wasp* and *Nashville* are hidden in the darkening haze. High above the *Barnstable County*'s superstructure, the ship's running lights describe an arc across the sky as the ship rolls.

Homecoming is starting to become real, and in a sense, threatening. "Debbie and I have both been through a lot, but separately, and we've changed," says Staff Sergeant North. "You start worrying: How is she going to be? How am I going to be? Is it going to be like it was before?"

On the one hand, says another Marine, "You can't wait to get home. On the other hand—and this is fucked up—but you don't want this to end."

The fantail considers that in silence. "Fucked up is right, man," someone says.

But there is general agreement at the idea. The bitching and complaining has ended, pushed away by something large, maybe a little mystical, but pure and real and solid. This is maybe the only meaningful thing in their lives; it defines them and gives them purpose, and value. They are Marines—not just military, but Marines, with a long history of sacrifice and glory. They volunteer, accepting the danger and the family separations and all the Mickey Mouse crap, and their service returns to them a deepening sense of values.

"Our values is what holds us together, and that's not a bullshit thing," a lance corporal says in the dark. "That's why I joined up, it's something I didn't want to miss. They stress values right from boot camp, it's like a brotherly thing. You work for a fire team, and everybody would do anything for anybody. Maybe that's hard for people who've never done it to figure out.

"When we were on libbo? My sergeant got shit-faced and he got beat up, and we got him back here and patched up. And in Somalia, everybody pulled together. You were terrified you'd do something to let your buddies down, or be responsible for getting somebody killed.

"So all the shit that sometimes goes on, you're pissed off at some guy or you resent somebody? All that disappears and you take care of each other.

"It's not something you have to do; it's something you want to do," he says. "The values are there, deep inside every Marine. It's something you hold on to for the rest of your life."

QUESTION: *Do you think the moral values of America (honesty, patriotism, willingness to sacrifice) are fading away, or are they still pretty strong?*

Fading fast! We are too soft. At times of national crisis we do well, but the crisis subsides and we are all lulled back into ourselves. We don't look out for our brothers, sisters, mothers, fathers, and most of all our old folks.
—Sergeant, Intelligence

[America's moral values] are still strong. I'm speaking from a black man's point of view. America has given minorities a raw deal, but I was born and raised here and still show patriotism. I do have a high moral standard, but that's due to my Christian beliefs. The U.S. service men and women are no more moral than any civilian.
—Sergeant, Infantry

13

ONSLOW BEACH
CAMP LEJEUNE, NORTH CAROLINA
August 1993

When the Marines arrive home at Camp Lejeune after a six-month absence, they don't just slip into town. They put on a show, a full-speed, balls-to-the-wall amphibious assault. At dawn, when the ships are still forty miles off the coast, *Wasp* launches her three Hovercraft, laden with men and vehicles and pallets. The Hovercraft bounce over the waves, their gas turbine engines propelling them at forty knots directly toward Onslow Beach on Camp Lejeune's Atlantic coast.

The mid-August sun is already baking the sand as the Hovercraft buzz over the horizon and roar up on the shore, slewing around to drop their ramps shoreward. Engines whine and gears clash as Humvees and trucks labor down the ramp and up onto the sandy beach road. Marines file off, rifles slung and seabags over their shoulders.

No one is there to see all this, except a couple of bus drivers waiting to take the Marines the few miles up the road to the barracks. There are no cheering families here, no welcoming banners snapping in the wind. Just sand dunes and a growing pile of gear.

This may be Homecoming Day, but it is a working day. Where work and family clash, family loses. Marines will work a full day and will be here for formation at 0730 tomorrow, as usual. Today, weapons will be returned to the armories. Vehicles will be washed down and backed into the storage bays vacated by the MEU that sailed a few days ago. And all the other gear—medical kits and stretchers, tents, cots, water cans, the few crates of spare parts that are left, footlockers, crates of administrative records, cartons of MREs—it all has to be sorted and stacked away, for in two days there will be an inspection.

The Marine Corps prohibits families from Onslow Beach, so they are gathered around the barracks area in a riot of banners and signs. Clusters of anxious wives and mothers and infants in strollers and grandfathers and daughters in their best Sunday dresses and ribbons in their pigtails. They are all in a lather of excitement and anxiety that starts to wear down as the sun rises higher and the sweat trickles and the morning drags toward noon and no Marines appear.

Here are Lou and Joan Silvestri, parents of Lance Corporal Erik Dacey. Joan wears a T-shirt with a message: "If You Think It's Tough Being a Marine, Try Being a Marine's Mom!"

"We've come to take him home," she says.

"He's done four six-month deployments in three years," says his father, a veteran. "He's supposed to stay on land for a while now, but you never know, I've been there."

And here is Vicky Fenton. The problems she crabbed about in her "smoker" to George a few months ago have been worked out. She got a house on base, a nice two-story colonial (in the lieutenant colonels' neighborhood) with a big, shady yard, and the kids can ride their bikes everywhere. "We moved over Memorial Day," she says, laughing at the memory. "The truck broke down so they had to move everything in pickups, and I spent about a month packing and unpacking and moving little stuff in the car." The Fenton kids skid up on their bikes. Eldest daughter, Kelly, hopes her father has found her a saxophone; probably he's been too busy.

"When are they coming?" she asks.

Now.

A truck grinds around the corner and squeals to a stop in the parking lot. Marines clamber off, grinning self-consciously. Families run, halt, shade their eyes. "Oh, it's Charlie Company," says the disappointed wife of a Bravo Company Marine. Jose Rocha searches for his wife, Karina, who's come up from Miami. Ron Tino finds his wife; she's got them a room at the Days Inn in Jacksonville. Mark Toal hugs his wife, Jackie.

Lou and Joan find Erik and wrap him in a wordless embrace: Home from Somalia. Safe!

Up the road, the wives have set up a blue-and-white-striped lawn tent. It shades a couple of garbage cans full of iced beer and soda and tables set out with pizza and cake. Scott Rogers's wife, Janet, sits on a folding chair nursing five-month-old Ashley Rene Rogers, born while Scott

Janet and Scott Rogers with baby Ashley.

was in Somalia. Heidi Poupard sits beside her; Heidi and Tim's three-year-old son, Mark, is trying surreptitiously to help himself to a soda.

The babble of excitement suddenly quiets at the distant buzz of a helicopter. The buzz grows more insistent and then it is here: One of the *Wasp*'s giant CH-53 helos thunders over the trees and churns in toward an adjacent parking lot. Before the families can even speak, they are struck by a gale of dirt, pebbles, twigs, and dust. Skirts blow up over faces; a balloon goes rocketing across the grass, followed by a pizza box and someone's jacket.

A corner of the tent trembles in the helo's whirlwind. It ripples.

George Fenton with (from left) Patrick, Jessica, and Kelly.

Someone yells above the din. Too late. The corner of the tent rips free, flaps fiercely, and then carries the rest of the tent with it. As the helo settles into a landing, the tent collapses in a swirl of poles and cake and blue-and-white-striped canvas.

Broderick emerges from the helo and hustles up the sidewalk toward his office. No one is here to meet him; his wife lives 250 miles away in Virginia, and he will drive there on the weekend.

Next comes George Fenton, grinning wildly. He is carrying his briefcase in one hand; in the other is a saxophone case. He is engulfed by his family.

Debbie North and daughter Brianna with Norman North.

Norman North finds Debbie and their daughter, Brianna; during the past six months she has grown from an infant into a walking, talking person, and she doesn't—maybe won't—recognize her dad. Norm sweeps her up anyway, hugging her with the purple stuffed toy he brought for her.

The tent is reerected, the tables set aright, and there is time for serious hugging and chatting before business begins again. Leave schedules are set out; most Marines will get eighteen days. Broderick will take a week. He will command the next six-month MEU deployment and is scheduled to leave in January. A skeleton staff has already begun work. Broderick has to figure out how to cram six months' worth of training into the next four months.

First, though, is politics. A call has come in from Washington that morning at 2:30 A.M., requesting that Broderick fly back to the *Wasp* to provide a tour for Senator Strom Thurmond, Republican of South Carolina (and ranking minority member of the Senate Armed Services Committee, which determines the Marine Corps budget). Thurmond also has

Debbie and Norman North, with daughter Brianna.

asked that Broderick muster on the *Wasp's* flight deck all the Marines from South Carolina, so that the Senator may greet them personally.

"Get fuckin' real," says a staff officer, looking around at the Marines hugging their children. Broderick agrees. He will helo out tomorrow to show the senator around, but he won't yank his Marines away from their jobs and families. Not even for the ranking minority member of the Armed Services Committee.

At 0730 the next morning, the Marines gather for formation. The sun is steaming the dew off the cropped grass. In a parking lot behind the MEU headquarters, Gunny Jerry Snodgrass forms up the command staff. "Uh ten . . . *huh!* Close interval! Dress heeriiiiight . . . *hress!* Puh . . . rade . . . *hress!*"

Broderick wades to the front of the formation.

He will never address them as a group again; after today, most will be transferred to other units, some will retire, some will go off to Marine Corps schools. A few will remain with Broderick for the next deployment.

George and Patrick Fenton.

Broderick has been with these men for twelve months. It has been intense, beginning with their first meeting in which Broderick had threatened to leave them behind in Somalia if they screwed up and endangered his Marines.

Broderick and his men have worked hard. Nobody screwed up and had to be left behind. On liberty, they played hard. They have performed extrordinarily well in an extraordinarily difficult mission, judging by the laudatory messages coming from headquarters.

Broderick is bursting with pride for his men. He thinks the Marines did accomplish something in Somalia. "The first time we were there we came out on a real high," he had said a few days ago. "In the areas where we operated, people got to live a normal life for at least the time we were there. We stopped the bandits, provided security in the city at night so people could walk around to the coffeehouses. Morale for the Somalis was way up, you could see it in their eyes. Kids lost that thousand-yard stare and started laughing and waving. These Marines showed that Americans are pretty good people, and I'm proud of every damn one of 'em.

"When we were called back in the second time, it was frustrating as hell. These guys wanted to play real bad, and having to just sit there was a kick in the rear end to their pride."

But Broderick measures success differently. He took 2,100 young Marines, lashed them into high-gear performance, and together they did a mission assigned by the commander-in-chief. They executed that mission flawlessly, and came home on schedule, without losing anybody. They even had a little fun.

Broderick's men are equally proud, although there are lingering doubts about their effectiveness in Somalia. "People have said our goal in Somalia was to contribute to the UN and try to help it become able to handle new security challenges," says Major Mike Dick. "We did that.

"But what are America's real strategic interests in this New World Order? There are parallels between today and 1947, when we had won World War II and before we got into the Cold War. Back then, you had Marshall and Kennan, big thinkers, guys who could think out where things were going.

"Where," asks Dick, "are today's big thinkers? I don't see any, and that concerns me."

Other senior Marines are simply relieved to be home.

"I was more concerned going into Somalia than into Kuwait during Desert Storm," says Gunner Grundy. "In Somalia, I simply didn't know

252

Matthew Broderick.

Matthew Broderick.

where the enemy was. The environment was more like Vietnam. The nights we'd launch off the *Wasp* in the dark, the smells and sounds, it brought back things from years ago. I was apprehensive.

"But we did well. The Marines were great. It all comes down to the values that we hold," says Grundy. "Everybody is human, we make mistakes, but we have these principles to guide on. The nation expects that of us, expects us to live by the principles of integrity, honesty, moral courage.

"And I think we will meet our mission as long as there are keepers of the flame," he says.

Broderick stands at attention in front of his men. He squints into the sun. There are several medals to be awarded. Gunny Snodgrass reads the commendations. Broderick steps forward, snaps a salute, and shakes each Marine's hand. Then he steps back, salutes again.

When the ceremony is over, Broderick wades off the field without a word. He is an intensely sentimental man. His love for these Marines is beyond expression. And anyway, Broderick is not given to expressing his sentiments aloud. But it has got to be done, and when the formation is dismissed, Broderick comes back.

He gathers his staff, a few at a time.

"I didn't wanna do this in formation, but I wanna personally thank you guys," he says to one group. "You're really professional Marines. You did a helluva job. You guys are shit-hot. You're important not only to me and to the Marine Corps but to a grateful nation. I'm gonna brag about you guys. Thanks, thanks a lot."

A half mile away the infantry grunts of the 24th MEU are standing in formation.

Eddie Adams and Jose Rocha and Chris Baron are standing stiffly at attention. Sergeant Major Roderick towers over them. Daryl Kyllonen and Erik Dacey and Donald Mortimer, Jon Flores and the rest of the Hell Bitch crew. And the company commanders, Tim Hederer and Mark Toal, all dead serious and ramrod straight.

They are the 1st Battalion of the 2nd Marine Regiment, and they are being addressed by their regimental commander, Colonel Thomas Jones. He has just told them they will work extra hours to get ready for the inspection.

"We ride you guys hard and put you away wet," he shouts to the sea of Marines.

"There's not many times to tell you how damned good you are.

"People in Hoboken or Toledo will never appreciate you. But so what? You are Marines and you can be proud of what you've done."

Okay, you asked so I shall let you have it. . . . I don't really believe the public knows what today's military is all about. They think we have it made. Free housing, free medical care, great retirement, everything paid for. . . . Last time I checked I still have car payments, bills, and the good old charge card bill to pay. I pay $650.00 a month for a nice home for my family. I pay for my dependents' (wife and children's) medical. . . . To sum it all up, I love my Corps and my country. I shall continue to do my job to the best of my ability. Why do I stay with it? HONOR, DUTY, COMMITMENT, LOYALTY and LOVE OF GOD, COUNTRY, CORPS.

—Sergeant, Aviation Technician

Epilogue

In January 1994, Matthew Broderick took the 24th Marine Expeditionary Unit back to Somalia.

Almost all the MEU's personnel were new: Its infantry grunts came from a different battalion, its pilots and aircraft mechanics from a different squadron. Of Broderick's top officers, only Lieutenant Colonel "Butch" Preston stayed on.

In the five months he had to get ready, Broderick rammed his new men through intense training at Camp Lejeune. For most of that time, Broderick worked and slept in his tiny office at the MEU headquarters building at Camp Lejeune. As fall passed into winter, he was persuaded to take a small bedroom in a converted WWII women's barracks.

The 24th MEU's assignment in Somalia was to guard the final withdrawal of American troops, who had been pinned down in a few heavily defended enclaves as chaos in Mogadishu accelerated. Except for a small security detachment, Broderick's Marines were the last American military personnel to leave; as they waded into the surf March 25, Somali looters poured into abandoned American positions.

During the fifteen-month U.S. intervention, forty-four Americans died in Somalia, thirty of them in combat. The American casualties made up about half of all UN peacekeeper deaths.

It was expected that the withdrawal of U.S. troops, including the intelligence and logistics specialists on whom the United Nations effort depended, would cause the final collapse of the humanitarian intervention. It was expected that neither the United States nor the United Nations would undertake similar interventions in the near future.

Just before Broderick left for Somalia, the White House nominated him for promotion to brigadier general. He was one of the fifteen selected from the Marine Corps's 627 colonels for promotion. Approval by the Senate would follow.

Meanwhile, the Marines in this book were detached from the 24th MEU, and most were thrown immediately back into the hectic pace of garrison life—exercises, inspections, maintenance, training. The routine was interrupted only once: On October 15, 1993, two months after their return from Somalia, several hundred of them were flown to the U.S. Navy base at Guantanamo, Cuba, standing by for insertion into Haiti. They were not needed. Three days later, they flew back to Camp Lejeune. Jerk-ex.

Norman North was informed in the fall of 1993 that he had been selected for promotion to warrant officer. That highly coveted honor (about 150 of 2,000 applicants are selected each year) threw the North household into a tizzy. North had been assigned to be a recruiter in Cincinnati. Debbie had bought a house there; their furniture was in storage awaiting the move. But North's promotion required him to attend warrant officers' school at Quantico, Va, starting in March 1994. Debbie put the Cincinnati house back on the market and moved back to Lejeune, where they rented a home in Jacksonville. There, she and their young daughter are living temporarily while they await Warrant Officer North's new assignment.

Having been away for six months of 1993, North had been looking forward to a quiet family Christmas at their new home in Jacksonville. Instead, he drew Christmas duty. He spent Christmas Eve and Christmas morning at the MEU's headquarters at Camp Lejeune.

Mark Toal was given command of Weapons Company at Camp Lejeune. In late winter 1994, he took his company to Alaska for winter training. In the subzero temperatures, his men found themselves wishing they were back in the baking sun of Somalia.

Lieutenant Colonel George Fenton, Broderick's operations officer, was selected to attend the U.S. Naval War College in Newport, R.I. His daughter, Kelly, plays first saxophone in the high school band. Youngest son Patrick still wants to grow up to be a Marine.

Lieutenant Larry Gill was assigned as a target information officer with the 31st MEU in the western Pacific. He occasionally rereads the detailed diary he kept while on patrol in Mogadishu, to remind him of the friends he made among the city's forlorn street children, and to remind himself that much of the world's population endures lives of misery and desperation.

Harry Bass gave up his beloved artillery company, Sierra Battery, in April 1994. He was hoping for assignment to Marine Corps headquarters in Washington, D.C.

Sergeant Carl Chapman was promoted to staff sergeant and attended the Non-Commissioned Officers' Academy at Camp Lejeune.

Mad Dog Moore was promoted to captain in February. He flies helicopters out of the New River Marine Corps Air Station near Camp Lejeune.

Dave Tierney pilots Harriers from the Marine Air Station at Cherry Point, N.C., where he is squadron operations officer. In the late winter and spring of 1994, his unit was on call to fly to Somalia, if necessary, in support of Broderick's 24th MEU.

Eddie Adams served as a rifleman in Charlie Company until the end of his enlistment term in late May, and hopes to become a minister. "I learned obedience and discipline in the military, and that really keys in with being a good Christian," he says.

Jose Rocha is stationed at Camp Lejeune, N.C., where he serves under Mark Toal in weapons company.

Jon Flores was promoted to sergeant. He oversees the operation and maintenance of the Hell Bitch and other light armored vehicles at Camp Lejeune.

In the weeks after Chris Baron got back from Somalia, he stubbornly clung to his hope that Alexandra, the lovely French girl he'd met and fallen in love with during liberty in France, would indeed come to visit.

In September, she came.

In a small ceremony near Chris's mother's house in Greenfield, Mass., they were married on September 21.

Chris completed his four-year term in the Marine Corps in March 1994. He and Alexandra set up housekeeping in Greenfield, where Chris is looking for a job.